ENDORS[...]

Working correctly with your angels, according to the Bible, can make the difference between life and death and fulfilling your entire God-given destiny!

SID ROTH
Host, *It's Supernatural!*

Whew! This book is probably the most important, strategic, and knowledge-imparting one from a revelatory standpoint that I have read in a long time! Tim Sheets has captured the revelation knowledge we need concerning angelic assignments and assistance to win the battles ahead as the Ekklesia. It took me forever to get through the book because I kept taking notes. I cannot remember when I have done that in the recent past concerning a book I've endorsed. I couldn't set it down! I'm buying the first copy, with pen in hand, marking it up like crazy and taking notes! This is a must-read if we want to win the battle before us. And we will! Great job, Apostle Tim Sheets.

BARBARA J. YODER
Lead Apostle, Shekinah Regional Apostolic Center
Breakthrough Apostolic Ministries Network
www.shekinahchurch.org
www.barbaraYODERblog.com

My favorite parts of Tim Sheets' book *Angel Armies on Assignment* are the decrees written at the end of every chapter. Job 22:28 says, "He will hear you and you will also decide and decree a thing." These decrees are ones we can take and use as we step into a breakthrough. Our breaker Lord is on the move, and this book is a tool for us to come into agreement as we watch what God and His angels will do.

BENI JOHNSON
Bethel Church
Redding, California
Author of *The Happy Intercessor, The Joy of Intercession,* and *The Power of Communion*

Sadly, I believe most Christians think more about demons than angels. Only a third of the angels fell, however, meaning there are at least twice as many angels as demons unless our Creator God made a few billion more angels! It will greatly encourage your faith as you learn of these celestial beings and the ways in which they have been assigned to assist you. And no one does a better job of explaining and enlightening us to this than Tim Sheets—no one.

This is an outstanding book!

DUTCH SHEETS
Bestselling author of *Intercessory Prayer* and *Appeal to Heaven*

I consider Tim Sheets the expert on the subject of Angel Armies. This insightful book equips us to win strategic heavenly victories and advance God's Kingdom in the earth as we cooperate with the angelic host. This is a book for these most important times.

JANE HAMON
Vision Church @ Christian International
Author of *Dreams and Visions, The Deborah Company, The Cyrus Decree,* and *Discernment*

For many years I have gleaned from the wisdom of Dr. Tim Sheets. His practical way of bringing understanding to supernatural concepts has created a pathway for me and many others to follow. In my own personal journey of understanding the angelic realm, I have often found confirmation in Dr. Sheets' writings, and I believe you will too. Whenever God desires to introduce a greater glory into the earth, He will speak through His ministers to build a spiritual framework in which He can release His purposes. In this day, the Holy Spirit is highlighting the importance of the present-day ministry of angels, including those that help to bring revival and increase our evangelistic witness. This is a biblical revelation that must be understood. In recent days, I, along with many others, have written books about the ministry of angels because it is a vital part of what God is doing in the earth today. And now, once again, Dr. Tim Sheets offers us another scripturally sound guide to move us further along in our understanding. This is an anointed book with many great lessons that must be grasped if we want to be used by God in the present-day shifting spiritual landscape. Read this book, apply this revelation, and witness *Angel Armies on Assignment*.

Joshua Mills
Bestselling author, *Seeing Angels* and
Encountering Your Angels
www.joshuamills.com

In these times of clear increased conflict in the spirit world, we need to know how to engage and agree with angelic powers. As a well-respected leader said to me, "God said darkness would degenerate into gross darkness, but tell My people I am sending My angels." God sending His angels and us agreeing with them in their engagement are two different things. Tim Sheets grants us insight into this endeavor. This book is not just a nice thing to have; it is imperative to the times we live in. Read it with much sobriety and seriousness. We are making history and we need angelic help!

ROBERT HENDERSON
Bestselling author of *The Courts of Heaven* series

Tim Sheets' book *Angel Armies on Assignment* is the must-read book for "such a time as this." While I have always admired his work, this book hit a "hope home run" for me personally and I know it will for you as well. The end isn't near, it's here and this book reminds us we are not fighting alone. We are resourced and empowered from heavenly realms right here on earth. Tim makes it clear the church is not a cruise ship; it's a battleship meant to go behind enemy lines and rescue POWs from the grip of satan. If you want to access the power of angelic forces all around you to break down strongholds and fulfill your end-times purpose, the practical insights and impartations Tim shares in this book will take you from wimp to warrior. Come on aboard!

TROY BREWER
Author *Redeeming Your Timeline*

ANGEL ARMIES
ON ASSIGNMENT

ANGEL ARMIES

ON ASSIGNMENT

The Divisions and Assignments of Angels and
How to Partner with Them in Your Prayers

TIM SHEETS

DESTINY IMAGE® PUBLISHERS, INC.

P.O. Box 310, Shippensburg, PA 17257-0310

"Promoting Inspired Lives."

This book and all other Destiny Image and Destiny Image Fiction books are available at Christian bookstores and distributors worldwide.

Cover artwork by James Nesbit

James@JNesbit.com

Interior design by Terry Clifton

For more information on foreign distributors, call 717-532-3040.

Reach us on the Internet: www.destinyimage.com.

ISBN 13: 978-0-7684-5396-6

ISBN 13 eBook: 978-0-7684-5397-3

ISBN 13 TP Int'l: 978-0-7684-5399-7

ISBN 13 LP: 978-0-7684-5398-0

For Worldwide Distribution, Printed in the U.S.A.

1 2 3 4 5 6 7 8 / 25 24 23 22 21

DEDICATION

We could never do what we do without our family. Rachel, Mark, Madeline, Lily, Jude, and Jaidin Shafer—and Joshua, Jess, Joelle, Samuel, and Grace—you all take first place in our hearts and are the reason we press on to try to make a difference. You are the future, and our hearts' desire is that you always fully know Him, trust Him, and serve Him.

ACKNOWLEDGMENTS

The amazing "book team" we have assembled along the way of this journey has once again proven themselves to be invaluable. I am indebted to Katelyn Cundiff, Marie Fox, Rachel Shafer, and of course my wife, Carol, for the countless hours, days, weeks, and even months that they contributed to the completion of this book. They helped me put into text form the revelations and insights Holy Spirit has revealed to me regarding Angel Armies, corrected my punctuation and grammar, and gave us input from the perspective of the reader.

As always, I value and highly esteem our partners at Destiny Image and appreciate the confidence they have shown in me. To Larry Sparks, Tina Pugh, and Brad Herman—*thank you.*

To those who prayed for us along the way—we are grateful and blessed by your support.

CONTENTS

FOREWORD

When Apostle Tim Sheets wrote his pioneering book *Angel Armies* in 2016, this is what I shared:

> Apostle Tim clearly communicates the spiritual dynamic of the alignment of the angelic government in Heaven with the apostolic government on Earth. This is a *must* book for the times in which we are living. The promises and principles included in, and the benefits you will receive from, reading *Angel Armies* will surpass most tools that you could acquire to help you during this time. This is a book that will prepare you for the future and help you see and be victorious in the clash of Kingdoms around you!

One of the best books that I have read for this decade is also by Apostle Tim Sheets, *The New Era of Glory: Stepping Into God's Accelerated Season of Outpouring and Breakthrough!* In the foreword, I shared:

When God's manifest presence invades our daily lives, things change! We cannot remain the same. Either we will harden our hearts, as the Israelites did on many occasions, or we experience new *zoe* life. If we choose to allow God's presence to soften our hearts then we may see the power of God released in greater measure. We may catch a glimpse of the very atmosphere of heaven. We experience God! He longs to pour out His glory upon His people so that we may know Him. This experience is not just for us personally but for the harvest of souls the Lord would draw in through the magnetic influence His presence has on the lost.

As the Holy Spirit moves us toward becoming more Christ-like, the methodology of an old season will not propel us into the future. We need something new and fresh. We need a new glory. This is one of the wiles of the enemy—to hold us captive in the last manifestation of God. Therefore, we live in the past rather than move into the best that is ahead for our life. This is how religious spirits operate.

When we are moving in God's glory, angelic visitation occurs. In December 2017, I was chosen by the Lord for an angelic visitation. The first place I ever shared this visitation was at a regional gathering hosted by Apostle Tim Sheets. We must co-labor with the Host of Heaven when we are moving in the glory realm in the earth. We are the army of earth. The Host of Heaven interacts with us to bring His victory into the earth realm.

Now comes the incredible book for today, *Angel Armies on Assignment!* This book is amazing! This book is interactive! There is a divine understanding of the supernatural realm of the Angel Armies, the Divine Person of Holy Spirit, and *you!* In this new era, the Spirit of God is developing a wineskin for an explosive Kingdom movement! Just as recorded in the book of Acts, we have entered a historic time of angelic manifestations. *Holy Spirit is mankind's advocate in the earth. However, angelic interaction comes in increased ways as Holy Spirit intervenes in our lives and takes liberty.*

In John 14:16, the Aramaic word describing Holy Spirit is not *advocate,* as in the Greek, but a combination of two words spelled by the Hebrew letters *Pey-Resh-Kuf-Lamed-Aleph.* The first is a *pey* word, *praq,* meaning "to end, to finish, to save." The second is *la,* an Aramaic word meaning "the curse." Therefore, this combination of words signifies *The One* who *Ends the Curse* that was begun in my house. This is a time to shout that Holy Spirit breakthrough is coming! This book by Apostle Tim prepares you for a heavenly invasion.

When Heaven invades, we learn how to hear the Spirit of God and enter the new season that has begun! As we embrace the next move of God, we co-labor with angels and ministering spirits! *Angel Armies on Assignment* will help you understand this interaction. This will also cause a supernatural interaction and greater conflict with the demonic realm. As you read these pages, you will gain new vision to unlock this season's provision! You have a mission field that has been determined for your future. This book is a commissioning tool necessary as you go forth with joy and boldness.

In my book *Interpreting the Times*, I have a section on "Through to the New: Travail, Order, and Time" where I share our need for a new anointing to break open God's full purpose. The goal we should have in each transition of life is to make it from the ending of one season to the beginning of the next *new* season.

We are there—ending one season, but beginning a *new*. There are eight "new" issues to look for in our life as we move from one season to the next:

- *New identity*—Your new transformed personality will have the ability to overcome the mountains in the past season that stopped your progress.

- *New garments of favor*—Garments, favor, and identity all go together. May you overcome, radiate with favor, and have an entryway into new opportunities.

- *New relationships*—When the Lord is doing a new thing in us, we must evaluate all of our relationships.

- *New acts*—Through history, every time God is ready to do something new, new acts begin that demonstrate His power today. We must expect to see the Lord divinely intervene in our lives with signs, wonders, and miracles in each new season we enter.

- *New weapons for the war ahead*—With each new season we must reevaluate our armor.

- *New sounds*—Every new season and every movement is preceded by a new song.

- *New anointing*—The anointing breaks the yoke. The anointing makes us grow so that every confining weight falls from us.

- *New level of authority*—May you receive the ability to stand in dominion in the sphere of authority that you have been granted by the Lord.

With that being said, there's a pressing required to make it through the narrow place of transition. Transitions are challenging and can require we leave much behind. Sanctification means to set yourself apart so you are ready to move forward in God's purposes. Sanctification is a time of removal of impurities. These are exciting times! I desire to press through the narrow place and receive the new! Use this incredible tool that Apostle Tim Sheets has provided us to press into the new. *Angel Armies on Assignment* is key for your new assignment.

Dr. Chuck D. Pierce
President, Glory of Zion International Ministries
President, Global Spheres, Inc.

INTRODUCTION

New Year's Day, 2020. A new year, new decade, and new era was beginning. I was thinking about our world facing one of its most defining moments. As I pondered world conditions I began to pray, "Holy Spirit, what is King Jesus saying to His church?" He responded with focused clarity that resonated deep in my spirit. It was a challenge to status-quo, passive Christianity. It was bold, decisive, and a call to exercise aggressive faith. "Tell My Ekklesia to raise the bar and I'll raise the anointing. Raise the bar and I'll pour out a fresh, new Pentecost greater than Acts 2."

"Raising the bar" is a term that is used in the Olympics. The high jumpers or pole vaulters leap over a bar, and if the bar is cleared it is then raised. This continues until someone clears the highest level and wins the gold medal. This phrase is now used in our times to refer to going to a higher level. I knew Holy Spirit was calling out to the true Ekklesia, the reigning church of spiritual governing authority in Jesus' Name, to raise the standard, to raise our faith and take genuine New Testament living to another level, to engage in prayer using spiritual weapons of warfare that are not natural—they are mighty through God to the destruction of anti-Christ strongholds.

The call of Heaven couldn't have been clearer. The true church of King Jesus must take its efforts to preach the gospel of His Kingdom to a new level. "When My heirs raise the bar, I'll raise the anointing and pour out a new Pentecost that will be greater than the outpouring in the book of Acts."

As I meditated and prayed into this call of Holy Spirit, I began to see amazing purpose and the prophetic destiny He has planned for the true Ekklesia of King Jesus. The Ekklesia is a spiritual legislating body ruling and reigning with Him in His Name. The remnant warriors in Christ's spiritual Kingdom are here to affect the natural kingdoms of the earth, regulating cultures, societies, laws, and discipling nations. I began to see the prophetic destiny of the real Ekklesia, functioning in a Holy Spirit-planned purpose for the decades to come.

There has never been anything like it before. All the anointings poured out since the birth of the church, all the vital streams revealing Heaven's truths to man will now flow together and synergize in power. This will all be soaked in a baptism of power from on high. A new Pentecost, with all its precedents, is going to another level. "Holy Spirit has brought us to a fullness of time. He is summing it up in our times as described in Ephesians 1. Under Holy Spirit supervision they will multiply in production, energy, and power. Operations, actions, strength, and function are going to multiply. Far more than ever has been done in church history will be done in our times."[1]

Please know Holy Spirit has planned our times well. Lucifer, the forever loser, is not a better planner than Holy Spirit. Not even close! Holy Spirit is a far superior strategist, engineer, and leader than satan ever thought about being. The meticulous detail He is bringing to the days ahead should fill us with hope and confidence. As has always been the case, He knows what He is doing. He has thought it through. It is nonsensical to think the designer of the universe missed something. His brilliance will expose an inferior kingdom of darkness and will reveal God-led plans for His people to win tremendous victories.

Those plans are now unfolding in times He's prepared. Breakthroughs of healings, miracles, resources, and harvests are on the horizon. Hell will not stop Him as He guides the Ekklesia into paths leading into the greatest days in church history. The New Testament church of Christ's Kingdom will see and live in times Holy Spirit spoke to me about years ago concerning angels saying, "The greatest days in church history are not in your past; they are in your present and your future!" That is His plan and He knows how to do it. Remnant believers in Christ must trust that emphatically and act accordingly. It's time for the radical remnant to follow Holy Spirit to another level.

Revelation for prophetic destiny is similar to putting a puzzle together. You connect one piece to another, and as you do the picture begins to manifest. It's like solving a riddle—contemplation is required. Often, direction and enlightenment for us individually, or the corporate body of Christ, occurs over spans of time as we ponder and pray into what God has said to us. Sometimes, words He spoke years ago or insight He has revealed in other seasons are pieces of the revelation that speak into our new times.

I believe God does it this way to keep us engaged with Him and from getting ahead of His timing. If He told us everything at once, we might just skip a few things and go straight to the end purpose. It's just human nature. This also allows time to grow our faith. The faith it takes to begin a prophetic journey is usually not enough to finish it. It must keep growing or purpose slows or stagnates. God, in His wisdom, has chosen to grow revelation as we grow our faith. In many ways, an enlightenment journey is also a relationship journey with the Lord, remembering what He has said and pressing into what He is saying.

The prophet Daniel is a great example of this. To understand his times, Daniel went back through the years and read the prophecies concerning the Babylonian captivity. He revisited revelations, visions, dreams, even angel visitations and messages. As he pressed in to seek the Lord with fasting and prayer, the revelation became clear. It's time! It's time for our captivity to end. The 70 years Jeremiah prophesied were ending. They were connecting to their moment.

This understanding enabled Daniel to pray and decree with such bold faith that two of Heaven's strongest angels, Gabriel and Michael, and the divisions of angels they command were sent by Holy Spirit to assist his intercession and bring it to pass. The battle lasted 21 days in the atmospheric and astrological heavens against the demon prince of Persia and his army. Heaven's angel armies won. Deliverance came just as God said it would.

Amazingly, the prayer of Daniel and God's people crying out for deliverance was answered by Holy Spirit activating two divisions of angel armies. They fought, assisting in releasing the grip of captivity of the Babylonian empire, the most powerful empire of that time. Their battle alongside God's people produced supernatural deliverance and reversed diabolical government conditions.

This, of course, was done under an old covenant. How much more should this partnership of the Holy Spirit and His angel armies, assisting God's very own heirs, function in a new and better covenant—one Jesus established through His cross. How much more should it operate in Christ's new Kingdom, assisting Christ's very own Ekklesia. Certainly, the bar has been raised. Hell has never faced what Holy Spirit has planned for His true Kingdom.

This was on the apostle Paul's mind when he wrote to the Hebrews concerning angels:

> *Are not the angels all ministering spirits (servants) sent out in the service [of God for the assistance] of those who are to inherit salvation?* (Hebrews 1:14 AMPC)

> *And if children, then heirs—heirs of God and joint heirs with Christ* (Romans 8:17 NKJV).

As children of God and joint heirs, we have inalienable Kingdom of Heaven rights. One of those rights is angel assistance. Angels are available to help us maintain our inheritance and, if need be, obtain deliverance and supernatural victories. It's time we operate in this proper Kingdom intention. We must do so at a much higher level if we expect to turn the captivity in nations and live in biblical freedoms. We must raise the bar.

NOTES

1. Tim Sheets, *The New Era of Glory* (Shippensburg, PA: Destiny Image Publishers, 2018), 58.

Chapter 1

ANGELS AND THE KING'S ADVANCE

Recently, I was pondering and seeking the Lord for strategies for our times in this new era. A constant prayer of mine is, "What is the present word of the Lord?" I was contemplating Holy Spirit's move in this new era with His angel armies and the remnant now forming an active Ekklesia, a reigning church moving in power and glory under greater authority than we have ever seen.

I began to pray about this in the spirit, using my heavenly prayer language. As I prayed, I began pondering the very first Ekklesia Jesus ever built in Acts 2, and I began to see many of the precedents initiated in the first Ekklesia now beginning to build in our times.

Then, and this is a bit unusual for me, I began to interpret what I was praying in the spirit. This was in a private time of prayer, not a corporate time. The ending part of what I interpreted was the apostles' prayer in Christ's first Kingdom Ekklesia in Acts 4:29. It rose up out of my spirit: "Grant that great boldness would be upon us to preach Your Word and give us signs, wonders, and miracles in the Name of Jesus." I just kept repeating that. The first Ekklesia in Christ's Kingdom prayed for boldness to confront adversarial culture, government, and religion, and we certainly need a similar anointing today.

Perhaps you've noticed there's a lot of animosity currently directed at the true church. Our values are demeaned and ridiculed by much of society. Some have even called us deplorables, misguided, needy, and poorly educated. The church has been pronounced as irrelevant and the demise of the church is often stated. We've even seen violence come against some churches and God's people have become targets of lawsuits for standing for their faith.

The climate is one of persecution if the church tries to use its influence. Don't get involved outside the four church walls. Don't speak into culture; don't speak into government. Be quiet. Be passive Christians who just stay out of things. I know so many who have accepted that. I actually have friends who have accepted that, but it's cross-grained with everything inside of me. Three songs and a sermonette have produced Christianettes.

I was pondering all of this and began to pray the prayer of the first apostles in the first Ekklesia. God, give us boldness to speak Your Word like never before. Boldness to declare what Your Word says without any compromise. I especially like how *The Message* records their prayer:

> *"And now they're at it again! Take care of their threats and give your servants fearless confidence in preaching your Message, as you stretch out your*

> *hand to us in healings and miracles and wonders done in the name of your holy servant Jesus." While they were praying, the place where they were meeting trembled and shook. They were all filled with the Holy Spirit and continued to speak God's Word with fearless confidence* (Acts 4:29-31).

After praying, "Lord, give us bold, fearless confidence to declare Your Word. Give us miracles, signs, and wonders," I then stated a very simple prayer, "Holy Spirit, what are You saying to the church? What are You doing right now?"

Usually, there is a period of seeking and pressing in before I get clarity. Normally, I spend several hours, even days, listening and contemplating, but not this time. This time, Holy Spirit answered immediately and there was a boldness in His voice that I instantly recognized. There was actually a conviction and a determination in His voice that I could feel.

I was on my way to do a conference for Prophet Chuck Pierce at Glory of Zion. I remember it so clearly. Holy Spirit said, "We're preparing to show the world the strength of the Lord of Hosts. He is tired of His sons and daughters being bullied. The strong arm of the Lord will now be seen overpowering and defeating the forever loser through the awakened Ekklesia." (For the past five years, every time the Holy Spirit refers to lucifer or satan to me, He refers to him as the "forever loser.") This had my attention, to say the least.

It was like a prophetic download that just kept coming. It is amazing how Holy Spirit can instantly download revelation that is extensive. Sometimes, it's like trying to get a drink from a fire hose.

Holy Spirit continued with a bold voice inside of me, and I wrote as quickly as I could, "My Ekklesia is now entering the times when prophetic words are intersecting their moment in accelerated ways. Prophetic words are intersecting their fullness of time, their due season. They have come to their activation moment and their assignment will now accelerate forward."

This was similar to a word given to me June 20, 2017. I was awakened about three o'clock in the morning with Holy Spirit saying, "My Ekklesia is now entering a fullness of time. A fresh new Pentecost will now be poured out. The precedent set in its foundations will now be seen in the remnant, and everything in My Kingdom will now accelerate. Begin to decree that the apostolic precedents in My first Ekklesia will now accelerate."

Be encouraged; everything is accelerating. I know many do not see it because troubling times tend to fog it up, but in Christ's Kingdom it is building and building quickly. The people in Acts 2 did not see it initially, either. Remember, the first apostles themselves wanted to quit before receiving the power and fire of God.

BE ENCOURAGED; EVERYTHING IS ACCELERATING.

Some considered going back to their old occupations, but a world-shaking, world-shaping event happened as prophesied, and the same thing is happening in our times. The true church isn't fading away into the sunset. No, the precedent is clear. We're going from glory to glory as Paul said in Second Corinthians 3:18. This must somehow mean bigger and bigger, or better and better, or stronger and stronger. It cannot mean weaker and weaker until we crawl off of this planet like whipped puppies. I'm not crawling anywhere. Like Shadrach, Meshach, and Abednego, I will not bow.

Our King and our brilliant strategist, Holy Spirit, have the greatest days in church history planned. Holy Spirit said prophetic words are connecting to their moment, thousands of them. Then Holy Spirit continued with a prophetic declaration that surged inside of me, saying:

Prophetic words have now intersected their moment, and the Ekklesia (New Testament church) must activate them with decrees of faith. As they do, angels of Christ's Kingdom government that I have now moved to the battlefronts will assist the Ekklesia's decrees to produce rapidly. Production in the Kingdom of God will now accelerate. I will empower their decrees and they will come to pass. You have entered the new day. A new era is before you. I will now reveal My hidden remnant. I have issued the call to millions in the secret place. Come from your caves, come from your dens, come from your hiding places. I am now revealing My hidden remnant and activating My glorious Ekklesia in fresh new ways. I will now activate the second apostolic age. It is an assignment of the new era. The second apostolic age will now aggressively rise.

In all honesty, I wasn't expecting that kind of passion or declaration. *In this era, I will activate the second apostolic age.*

This will be an age of supernatural boldness. I recently received this dream from Gina Gholston, a prophetic dreamer from Clarksville, Tennessee, concerning boldness.

I just returned from Billye Brim's prayer conference in Branson, Missouri. I opened my Facebook tonight and saw that you, Dutch, and Ken Malone were having meetings in Florida and that the conference was called the Backbone Summit. My jaw dropped when I read this title because I was immediately reminded of a dream I had on March 30, 2019. In this dream, I was standing in an operating room. I saw in front of me an operating table, but at the head of the bed where the pillow should have been was a hole, and that struck me as odd. I knew it was set up like this for a purpose.

As I was looking at that operating table, two men came in through the door holding up and leading a man into the OR. The man looked old and decrepit and was in major pain. He was grimacing and his body was shaking from pain and agony. He had on regular clothes, jeans and a shirt. They led him to and laid him on this operating table face down. His face was positioned in the hole where the pillow should have been.

I then noticed that his shirt did not have a back on it. His back was exposed, but instead of a normal back, there was a huge gaping wound from his neck down to his hips. As I looked at that wound, I saw that he did not have a backbone. It was as if it had been removed and he was left with the agony of the effects of that open wound and spineless condition.

I then noticed the two men who brought him into the OR had left the room, but the doors opened again and they came back in, carrying a brand new backbone. It was a real skeletal backbone. I knew this was why we were in this OR. This was what all this had been for. They were giving this man a backbone.

They took the new backbone and placed it in the opening on the man's back. When they did, the wound was immediately healed and the man stood up straight and tall and walked out the doors. He was not old and decrepit as he had initially appeared. He was a young man. He was instantly strong and vibrant. He was renewed, restored, revolutionized. He had received a backbone.

A few days later, the Lord said to Gina, "My church has appeared to be old and decrepit, fallen into ruin and disrepair, but I have brought you to a season of restoration. I have prepared this moment. I have put a backbone in My church, My Ekklesia, and they will stand up straight, strong, vital, courageous, and revolutionized. This will change everything."

What a glorious moment we are in. God has led us to a Holy Spirit-planned moment and He is strengthening His body to stand in power, with courage, and display a new backbone. We will advance and prevail. Hear the word of the Lord:

It is time for the surge of My Kingdom. I will now rise and lead My people through gates of awesome breakthrough. I will break all confinements. Hear the sound of confinement breaking. Hear the sound of angels of breakthrough scattering and shattering confinement at My command. Economic, government, religious, and demonic confinement, break.

For the forces of My Kingdom have been prepared to initiate the advance, and My angels have heard the command—begin the advance, remove the obstacles, and open the glory roads for the advance.

My Holy Spirit has prepared strategies and is now moving angel army divisions to the battle. My Ekklesia has been aligned. I have tuned the voice of My apostles and prophets. I am leading the advance of My Kingdom. I have never led a retreat, a defeat, or a stalemate. I lead advances, victories, and deliverance. I am rising to lead My Kingdom in the magnificent advance that is promised. I am standing to lead the breakout.

Hell's kingdom will now experience might it cannot withstand. Overwhelming force will now come to bear upon diabolical structures of darkness. Evil and deep-rooted iniquity will be uprooted by My advancing Kingdom. Warrior champions are rising to follow Me in unrelenting purpose, aggressive faith, and bold declarations. The world has not experienced aggressive power like I will now release through My remnant.

For the generational winds are blowing in synergy. They are driving My march to change history. Evil empires will crumble. Evil structures will fall. Evil philosophies will be destroyed by truth. Evil roots deep within this nation will be exposed and destroyed by the faith decrees of My Kingdom.

Hear the sound of Heaven. Hear the sound of fresh winds of Pentecost. Hear the sound of marching. Hear the sound of shoutings from radical remnant faith warriors. Hear the drums of the conquering King beginning to beat. Their resounding message is now resonating in the core of My remnant.

My Holy Spirit is stirring their hearts with My heart. They will now press with Me into supernatural breakthrough. Miraculous turnarounds and explosive change will now break through. Bondage will suddenly break, and brand-new life and freedom will witness that My liberating force has come through their doors.

Yes, I am rewriting the story of the downcast, bruised, forsaken, wounded, and the captives. Their witness of Me shall be My declaration through the ages. I am the Lord mighty to save. I am the Breaker. I am the God of Breakthrough. I will now rewrite your story. I will now rewrite the story of this nation. I will march when I want to march. I will go wherever I want to go and I will do whatever I want to do.

The attempt of the forever loser and his kingdom to resist Me will be futile. I have set My face and I will not relent. My remnant and Ekklesia will break through. Strongholds of hell will scatter and shatter. Glory that dispels darkness will shine. Do not faint, quit, turn back, or become passive. Advance with Me and My Kingdom. Advance under Holy Spirit anointings. Advance with My angel armies. Enter, by faith, the new season of breakthrough and you will birth breakthrough after breakthrough after breakthrough.

Listen and you will hear the sound of awesome winds of change. Four quarter winds of change are blowing. For I have heard the cries of "how long," I have heard the cries against delays. You shall surely now enter your due season. My appointed time has come. My winds are shifting conditions in your favor. My power is shaking the heavens and the earth. Know that the great shaking will result in your favor.

It is a shaking that shakes doors open, reveals hidden riches, and uncovers your inheritance. It is a shaking that breaks chains of bondage, setting you free. You will be free. I will break you free. You will now see the change that I have planned. Look for it and step forward into it. You will now see the change from wilderness wandering to awesome times of transitions into promised places, times, and dreams of your heart. Your conditions will change as you transition into abundance.

My winds of change will blow upon My remnant. They will blow upon My church. Miraculous change will be seen manifesting to displace barrenness.

I am ending the barren times of My people. I am ending the dark, barren times hell has propagated against My church. I am releasing the fresh winds of a new Pentecost, and that wind will blow darkness away. It will blow away the barren times, the strategies of darkness, and obstacles to My blessings. It will blow down the obstacles to cultural, academic, government resistance, and deceitful barricades of humanism and lawless propaganda will fall. It will blow down the anti-Christ activism meant to harass you.

I am sending the winds of change. Lift up your eyes and look with expectancy. Lift up your voice and declare with expectancy. Lift up your hands and worship with expectancy. I am changing the season. I am sending transformation winds. I am soaking you with favor. I am freeing you to rise up with wings like eagles and soar on Holy Spirit winds. I am freeing you to run and not grow weary, to walk and not faint. I am empowering you to pass through the floods and not be harmed, to pass through the fire and not be burned.

You will now enter the calving season of hopes, dreams, and confessions of faith. Let your heart embrace it. Let your soul embrace it. Let your mind embrace it. Miraculous winds of transformation are now blowing. Holy Spirit's anointing is being poured forth and the divisions of angel armies are coming to assist you.

Welcome to the second apostolic age. Welcome to the season of raising the bar.

DECREES

1. WE DECREE an anointing of boldness is rising in the body of Christ.

2. WE DECREE passive Christianity is changing to government declarations of faith.

3. WE DECREE against fear and say confidence will rise.

4. WE DECREE everything in the Kingdom of God is accelerating.

5. WE DECREE Holy Spirit has the greatest days in church history planned.

6. WE DECREE all prophetic words are coming to their moment of activation in Jesus' Name.

7. WE DECREE the forever loser and his kingdom are bound in Jesus' Name.

8. WE DECREE the remnant are coming out of their hiding places.

9. WE DECREE we are going from glory to glory to glory.

10. WE DECREE break up, break out, breakthrough, passover, and possess.

Chapter 2

MESSIAH THE BREAKER AND BREAKTHROUGH ANGELS

I woke up on Passover morning (April 8, 2020) and was blind in my right eye. I couldn't see anything, not even my hand in front of my face. Nothing like this had ever happened to me, and amazingly I wasn't all that upset or fearful. I had so much to do that day and I just wanted to get on with it. We were filming, I had conference calls and prayer service to prepare for, and I was simply thinking this was a hassle!

My wife, Carol, said I needed to see a doctor and find out what was going on. I agreed that was probably wise, and when I called they advised me to get to an emergency room because I could be having a stroke. I thought, "No, I'm not having a stroke. I know I'm not." I didn't go, and in the meantime we got hold of a friend who worked for an optical office who was able to get me an appointment for later that day at the Cincinnati Eye Institute.

After running various tests for several hours, they determined I had a virus in my eye and gave me four prescriptions. The next morning, as I was getting ready for some podcast interviews in my office, I was praying and talking to the Lord when a thought crossed my mind: "I wonder if this is prophetic?" This had been so unusual. I knew God hadn't done this to me, but I was wondering if He wanted to speak to me through this.

I said, "Holy Spirit, do You have something to say to me concerning the vision of the apostolic or prophetic being attacked?" As soon as I prayed that, I was instantly in the spirit. I don't even know how to describe it, but if you have ever had it happen you know it's as if you just stepped into a different realm. I could see things in the spirit.

The apostle Paul taught that the Greeks always believed that the spirit realm was more real than the natural because the spirit realm is eternal, while the natural is only temporary. In actuality, both realms are real; it's like a parallel universe. Particle physics tells us there are 11 different dimensions. It's like getting a drop of water out of a pond, which you drop onto a glass slide and view through a microscope. Suddenly, you see there's a world going on in that drop of water that you didn't see with your natural eyes. It was always there, but you had to have the right equipment to see it. The same is true of the spirit realm. It is very real, but only Holy Spirit can anoint you to see into it. He does this through a gift described in First Corinthians 12 as the discerning of spirits.

I began to see a vision in the spirit realm that I had seen many times over the last couple of years—of breakthrough angels that accompany Messiah the Breaker. There are millions of these breakthrough angels in this division. Micah 2:13 says Messiah the Breaker will go before us and we will break through. When Jesus went to the cross, He said He had 72,000 (six legions) of these angels with Him, and if He wanted to break out of this He could, but He submitted to the plan of God. Clearly, breakthrough angels accompany Him.

I saw them in Vancouver, Red Deer, St. Thomas, and in various places throughout America as well as at The Oasis. Each angel carried what looked like a long wooden mallet, similar to a sledgehammer. They would strike the ground, hitting it so hard I could feel the thud of it. You could feel the vibrations as the angels struck the ground, making their decrees of *"Break up! Break out! Break through!"* They repeated this over and over.

One particular Sunday morning at The Oasis, I saw breakthrough angels lined up around the sanctuary, striking the ground with huge wooden mallets. Our worship leader, who is my daughter, Rachel, was singing a song of the Lord at the time: "One, two, three, four, as they strike the ground, He's breaking open doors." I saw an enormous angel to my right holding out a huge mallet. When I turned back, I saw many other angels around the sanctuary striking the ground with their mallets declaring, "Break up, break out, break through."

At this point, Rachel transitioned to the next song and began singing, "When He walks into the room." At that point, the huge angel to my right put his mallet down by his side and the other angels, seeing him do this, put their mallets down by their sides and bowed their heads in reverence to the

Breaker. Of course, these actions signified their understanding that the important One is the Breaker Himself. They are just serving Him to bring us breakthrough. At this point, I felt the atmosphere of the room shift completely, and as the tangible presence of the King Himself came into the room I began to weep. I was recognizing how much these angels were reverencing the Lord Jesus, our Breaker. There is absolutely nothing like the presence of the Breaker Himself, not even the presence of angels. When the King comes in, everything changes.

On the morning I was asking the Lord about the loss of my eyesight, I saw in the spirit realm a host of these same breaker angels. This time, however, Holy Spirit added two more words to what the angels had decreed before. I believe this is prophesying into our times because this was during Passover. This time, the angels were striking the ground and decreeing, "Break up. Break out. Break through. Passover. Possess."

I had never heard Holy Spirit have the angels use these two words in this way—*passover* and *possess*. I began to understand a major shift is taking place in the spirit realm. The Breaker Himself and His Holy Spirit have plans, and His angels are being activated and are going forth into this world to break up, break out, break through. They are enabling us to passover and possess our inheritance. They are being released by the millions upon this planet to assist us in awesome breakthrough.

It is our time to break out and passover into an inheritance in new ways at new levels. We've come into a fullness of time—meaning prophetic words, dreams, and visions are now connecting to their moment. Our prayers are hitting the mark; they have been heard and Heaven is answering. The

Ekklesia is being seated with an anointing to prevail. They are being seated with Christ's authority, declared from their lips at levels the world has never seen before. There is boldness and their decrees of faith are being heard, activating and permitting some things on earth and deactivating or forbidding others. We're entering seasons of supernatural breakthrough. They will happen in your life and in churches everywhere.

At the end of hearing the angels of breakthrough decree, "Break up. Break out. Break through. Passover. Possess," I then heard a starting pistol being fired like you would hear at the beginning of a race. In high school, I ran track, and at the beginning of a race you hear a starting pistol. No one shouts *run*; the pistol itself prophesies *run*. It is time to run with King Jesus. It's time to run into breakthrough, to run to the battle and see the success we have been promised. It's time to run with Messiah our Breaker.

> *The One who breaks open the way will go up before them; they will break through the gate and go out. Their King will pass through before them, the Lord at their head* (Micah 2:13 NIV).

> *Then I, God, will burst all confinements and lead them out into the open. They'll follow their King. I will be out in front leading them* (Micah 2:13).

> *The Breaker [the Messiah] will go up before them. They will break through, pass in through the gate and go out through it, and their King will pass on before them, the Lord at their head* (Micah 2:13 AMPC).

> IT'S TIME TO RUN INTO BREAKTHROUGH,
> TO RUN TO THE BATTLE AND
> SEE THE SUCCESS WE HAVE BEEN
> PROMISED. IT'S TIME TO RUN
> WITH MESSIAH OUR BREAKER.

Please notice King Jesus is identified as King Breaker who goes before us to ensure our breakthrough. He leads us through "gates," which is the Hebrew word *shaar*, which means "doors" (Strong's H8179). Doors to new areas, opportunities, places, or lands. It represents a way through.

Jesus is the way opener. He goes before His people to break up obstacles, opening the way to new promised territories, inheritance, and destiny (both individual and corporate). The one who plans your destiny goes before you, breaking you free from any hinderance to that destiny.

The word *breaker* is the Hebrew word *parats* and it means "to break out, to burst out, to grow out, to grow through something" (Strong's H6555). It's like a seed that grows up out of the dirt and, as it does, it will break out and produce what it is. It's similar to a child who grows out of his/her clothes. This kind of breakthrough comes as a result of growth. You grow up and out.

Also, *parats* means to increase in spiritual strength until you're strong enough to break something. *Parats* means "the one who breaks up, goes before to give you strength to breakthrough." Breakthrough is the Hebrew word *abar* and it means passover or crossover (Strong's H5674). According to Hebrew scholar Spiros Zodhiates, *parats* can also mean to impregnate with concepts, ideas, or purposes. *Parats* means the seed is planted and it goes through the growth process. It is nourished in the womb, then it breaks out of the womb and passes through to new life in the world, where it can grow and become who or what it is.

Although there are many types of breakthrough, let me reference three of them for you:

- **Suddenly**. Some breakthrough is simply the busting up of situations or hinderances, etc. God comes, He breaks it up, and you're free. It's a suddenly.

- **Grow your way out of**. Other breakthroughs you must grow your way out of, with His assistance. To achieve supernatural breakthrough, you may have to acquire spiritual strength and growth to break out.

- **Impregnate your soul**. Some breakthrough comes from God impregnating your soul with something that you must nourish in the womb of your soul, until it's time for it to break out and live outside in the world.

I've seen all three types of breakthrough in my life over the years. If you've been a Christian for any length of time, you've probably experienced all three of these. There've been times when the Lord just simply broke things up and I was free. He busted confinement with the various means of His power at His disposal and I passed through.

There have been plenty of other breakthroughs where the Holy Spirit has helped me grow my way through. I had to strengthen myself in the spirit, growing my faith, getting rid of any areas of unbelief or any issues that I needed to, and then He led me to the doors of breakthrough. Like a seed, there have been times I've had to grow up through dirt and break forth into new strength so I could live in a new place that God wanted me to live in. It was more of a process of breakthrough that He led me through. As a result, I was able to produce in a new place at a new level.

Some breakthroughs have resulted in God impregnating my soul with possibilities, dreams, ideas, concepts, callings, and prophecies. All seeds have different gestation periods. For a woman, it is nine months. If you're raising tomatoes, you can get a crop in a few weeks, but if you're growing an oak tree, it's going to take a few years. It's the same with animals—a squirrel's gestation period is about 45 days while an elephant's is 18 months.

In the spiritual realm, some dreams have a longer gestation period than others. There have been many times breakthroughs that God has given have come through, impregnating my soul with possibilities and dreams that I've had to nourish, feed, and protect until it was time for it to break through and live on the earth. Other times I had to raise dreams like you would raise a child.

These three types of breakthroughs occur in seasons of outpourings overseen by Holy Spirit, Jesus the Breaker, and assisted by breakthrough angels. We have cycled into a mega-Pentecost era. Power from Heaven is being poured out to break us out into new places, territories, inheritances, concepts, prophetic understanding, and destiny. New downpours of anointing from Heaven, greater than Acts 2, will soak the people of God in an anointing to prevail.

Micah 2:13 also says, "Then I, God, will burst all confinements." It is the season for confinement to break as Messiah the Breaker goes before us as His Kingdom advances. The confinements and constraints upon the true church are now going to be supernaturally broken. Millions of promises will now spring up and break free—no more confinement and no more delay. The breaker angels accompanying Him have heard the King's decree to break confinement. When we stop listening with our natural ears to what the world is saying and start listening with our spiritual ears, we will hear the chains of disease, poverty, fear, bondage, and depression break.

> *The Breaker [the Messiah] will go up before them. They will break through, pass in through the gate and go out through it, and their King will pass on before them, the Lord at their head* (Micah 2:13 AMPC).

Alah is the Hebrew word for "go up" and is used over 900 times in the Old Testament (Strong's H5927). It means to mount up, to rise up, to lead up. *Alah* also means to go from a lower elevation to a higher one. It pictures, in the Hebrew language, sheep being led by their shepherd to a higher feeding area. *Alah* compares to *anago*, which is the Greek word for "led up." *Anago* also means "to mount up, rise up, or to go to a higher elevation" (Strong's G321). In Matthew 4:1, we read that

33

Jesus was *led up* by the Holy Spirit to a mountain, where He fasted and prayed for 40 days, overcoming the devil's attack. Both Micah 2:13 and Matthew 4:1 are describing Jesus the Messiah. In the Old and the New Testaments, Messiah the Breaker is described as one who takes sheep to a higher level.

Anago and *alah* give clear prophetic meaning to us today. The identity of Messiah the Breaker prophesies to us that He will give breakthrough after breakthrough so that we can go to higher and higher levels in life, relationships, purpose, and ministry. There is a remnant with a willingness to follow the Breaker and come on up in order to advance Christ's Kingdom to a new level on the earth.

> THERE IS A REMNANT WITH A WILLINGNESS TO FOLLOW THE BREAKER AND COME ON UP IN ORDER TO ADVANCE CHRIST'S KINGDOM TO A NEW LEVEL ON THE EARTH.

Our King Jesus is rising now as Jehovah *Parats*, the Breaker, with Heaven's division of breakthrough angels. There are millions of these angels who will now assist Him to:

- Take His sheep to a higher elevation;
- Take us to higher feeding levels;
- Take us to deeper things in the Kingdom of God;

- Take us to new levels of the glory of His presence;
- Take us to new heights of praise and worship;
- Take us to higher levels of success in business and in every other area of life, spirit, soul, and body.

We're entering the seasons of supernatural breakthrough. They will happen in your life and in churches everywhere. The attacks against the prophetic and apostolic vision will backfire, just as they did with my eye. God is restoring clear vision, leading to the greatest harvest we have ever seen, confirmed by signs, wonders, and miracles.

As I studied and meditated on the Breaker anointing, an old song of revelation came to mind: "Higher Ground (I'm Pressing on the Upward Way)" by Johnson Oatman. Johnson Oatman was a layman preacher who ran a mercantile business and an insurance agency. He was also a prolific songwriter of the revivals in the 1800s. It's estimated that Oatman wrote between four to five songs per week, eventually penning over 3,000 songs, for which he was paid $1.00 each by a gospel publisher.

"HIGHER GROUND (I'M PRESSING ON THE UPWARD WAY)"

I'm pressing on the upward way,
New heights I'm gaining every day;
Still praying as I'm onward bound,
"Lord, plant my feet on higher ground."

Refrain:

> *Lord, lift me up and let me stand,*
> *By faith, on Heaven's tableland,*
> *A higher plane than I have found;*
> *Lord, plant my feet on higher ground.*
> *My heart has no desire to stay*
> *Where doubts arise and fears dismay;*
> *Though some may dwell where those abound,*
> *My prayer, my aim, is higher ground.*
> *I want to live above the world,*
> *Though Satan's darts at me are hurled;*
> *For faith has caught the joyful sound,*
> *The song of saints on higher ground.*
> *I want to scale the utmost height*
> *And catch a gleam of glory bright;*
> *But still I'll pray till heav'n I've found,*
> *"Lord, plant my feet on higher ground."*

The call of the King and the Holy Spirit is to press upward to higher levels of ministry, purpose, and a greater calling. The Messiah is leading us into a supernatural breakthrough season. Step forward by faith and believe that confinement is going to break off of your life. Press in and come on up to higher ground, into greater glory, worship, and destiny. As the song says, "My heart has no desire to stay where doubts arise and fears dismay...my prayer, my aim, is higher ground." Thankfully, we have millions of angels in the breakthrough division to assist us in going to higher ground. Assisting us to break up, break out, break through, passover, possess.

DECREES

1. WE DECREE Messiah the Breaker is going before us and we will break through.
2. WE DECREE doors to new opportunity are breaking open.
3. WE DECREE our prayers are hitting the mark.
4. WE DECREE that when the King comes in, everything changes.
5. WE DECREE dreams and visions are connecting to their moment.
6. WE DECREE that we are being anointed to prevail.
7. WE DECREE inheritance in new ways and at new levels.
8. WE DECREE suddenlies of Holy Spirit are breaking out around the world.
9. WE DECREE every strategy of hell will backfire.
10. WE DECREE break up, break out, breakthrough, passover, and possess.

Chapter 3

PENTECOST AND THE YOKE DESTROYING ANOINTING

When I received the vision of the breakthrough angels, I recalled what Prophet Chuck Pierce had prophesied in 2019 concerning a literal Passover that would occur in 2020. This happened; the entire world passed over a coronavirus pandemic, a literal plague.

Just as Moses had told the people to stay in their homes during the first Passover, Benjamin Netanyahu, the Prime Minister of Israel, announced in April, 2020 a nationwide lockdown during the end of the Passover holiday. And, just as Moses and the Israelites passed out of Egyptian bondage with the armies of the Lord accompanying them (see Exod. 12:41), we, too, are going to see the releasing of angel armies on assignment to break us through into new land.

As all of this was occurring, I heard Holy Spirit say to me, "Just as Passover will be a literal Passover, Pentecost will be a literal Pentecost."

Pentecost activates a yoke-destroying anointing so we can break out and break free. It doesn't just break the yoke, it destroys it according to Isaiah 10:27: "It shall come to pass in that day that his burden will be taken away from your shoulder, and his yoke from your neck, and the yoke will be destroyed because of the anointing oil" (NKJV). Something that is merely broken can be fixed, but God says, "My anointing *destroys* yokes."

A yoke is a wooden bar that fits over the neck of oxen, or other beasts of burden, and joins them with a leather strap, so they can work together. With the yoke in place, the oxen are used to plow through fields or to pull heavy wagons.

God says, "I'm going to pour out my anointing and destroy the yokes that have bound you. You're entering into a time when you won't have to plow everywhere you go or drag heavy burdens around with you. I'm activating a new Pentecost, and I'm going to release a deluge of anointing that obliterates yokes of bondage so My people can move into new territories of blessings, hope, and harvest."

Pentecost is all about God changing times and seasons. We see this in the life of Daniel who experienced the three types of breakthrough described in the previous chapter. For Daniel, some breakthroughs were suddenlies. God came, obliterated some things, and there was breakthrough. However, there were some breakthroughs Daniel had to grow up and out of. And in other breakthroughs, God impregnated Daniel's soul with dreams, visions, and prophecies that would grow as he stewarded them in the womb of his soul. This particular aspect of breakthrough is amazing to ponder—Daniel served with the king's eunuchs and had been surgically sterilized, resulting in an inability to produce in the natural realm. But God enabled him to be highly successful, or productive, in His Kingdom. Daniel was stating his faith that "God changes times of barrenness and cycles me into periods of high productivity."

This is a part of what the new Pentecost is about—an ability and an anointing enabling us to produce beyond the natural realm. We're not limited to natural abilities. Holy Spirit comes, activating divine ability, empowering us to do what we cannot do in and of ourselves. This particular season of Pentecost is also about God birthing some things on the earth that Holy Spirit has planned and that King Breaker and His breakthrough angels will lead us into.

God's Word teaches us that the first New Testament Pentecost in Acts 2 was about birthing—the first Ekklesia, the first Kingdom of God and government of Christ's heirs, a great move of God, an abundant harvest, the fivefold ministry, and activation of the saints to do the work of the ministry. The Pentecost we are now cycling into is the same—we are entering into a mega-birthing season. There are things that He has impregnated into His Kingdom that have now come to calving season; they are due.

In 2020, the entire world was facing a worldwide pandemic. COVID-19 was spreading around the globe, and I began to ponder the pause the world was being put into because of it. We had to put everything on hold, let it pass through, and then we could move forward. In prayer, I said, "Lord, there must be something significant in the spirit realm concerning what the whole world's focused on in the natural realm.

Holy Spirit, what is this pause prophesying and saying to the church?" As I began to pray in Holy Spirit language, I threw the switch and started listening with spiritual ears rather than with my natural ears.

I heard His answer as clearly as if you had walked up to me and said it. I heard Him say, "This time between Passover and Pentecost is a pregnant pause." I began to pray into that and to meditate on what that meant.

In the last few weeks of a pregnancy, you pause a bit, slowing down and not moving around as much. It's not because anything is wrong, but because it's right, and the time to deliver is close. You're waiting, but with expectancy. A pregnant pause is a pause preceding birth to strengthen and prepare what is about to be birthed. You could have a baby at six or seven months, but it would be fragile and would require a lot of care. Typically, if you can nourish the baby and rest the last few weeks of the pregnancy, the child will be born ready to thrive.

The dictionary definition of a pregnant pause can also refer to building anticipation for a declaration, a revealing of something, a mission or a goal that you wish to emphasize, or an answer to something. A pregnant pause signifies the importance of what is to be revealed, or the importance of a goal about to be stated or activated.

Pentecost is about birthing a movement and generating supernatural power that man doesn't have in and of himself. Prophetically, we have moved from a pregnant pause to a mega Pentecost. We will now see the birth of a new Kingdom of God movement on this planet like has never been seen before. All of the past moves are activating anew in a fresh anointing of the Holy Spirit to function at higher levels, along with all the new concepts, places, territories, and prophetic destinies that Holy Spirit has planned. This will all be done in a spiritual atmosphere of far greater glory.

There will never be a time when God's manifestation will be as clear as it will be now. The presence of God will be felt and seen. This will birth a functioning Ekklesia, one that has been trained and nurtured in the soul of a remnant. This Ekklesia is due to be birthed on this planet and is a game changer. We will stare hell in the face and not back down. We will see signs, wonders, and miracles that will activate the power of God on this earth at levels that have been ordained through the prophets. This is the purpose and the function of the second apostolic age.

We're moving from a pregnant pause to a worldwide revival that is being birthed to answer a global pandemic of sin, rebellion, and iniquity. Holy Spirit impregnated Christ's Kingdom with all that is needed for Messiah the Breaker to lead us through doors to His greatest move in all of history. He is supplying breakthrough angels to assist us in accomplishing His plans, and they will be released in this new-era Pentecost.

A remnant has been nurturing and strengthening those promises in the wombs of their souls, not letting it go. We've held on to them, fed them, and decreed them. They will grow to fullness, ripen, and be birthed. I believe that's why Holy Spirit allowed me to see into the spirit realm and observe the break-through angels that accompany Messiah the Breaker, who were declaring as they struck the earth, "Break up, break out, break-through, passover, possess." Those are the characteristics of the Breaker Himself, *Jehovah Parats*, King of Breakthrough, who passes before us to ensure our breakthrough.

We're going to see a breakthrough and a birthing of hopes, dreams, concepts, goals, promises, and visions. We've come to the time and Pentecost is coming to give us strength to deliver it. The strategies hell has attempted will now backfire. The apostle Paul said it brilliantly in Romans 8, writing these words at the end of his life:

> *With the arrival of Jesus, the Messiah, that fateful dilemma is resolved. Those who enter into Christ's being-here-for-us no longer have to live under a continuous, low-lying black cloud. A new power is in operation. The Spirit of life in Christ, like a strong wind, has magnificently cleared the air, freeing you from a fated lifetime of brutal tyranny at the hands of sin and death. God went for the jugular when he sent his own Son. He didn't deal with the problem as something remote and unim-portant. In his Son, Jesus, he personally took on the human condition, entered the disordered mess of struggling humanity in order to set it right once and for all* (Romans 8:1-4).

Please understand that Holy Spirit is going to, once again, enter the disordered mess with King Jesus and angel armies and, with a functioning Ekklesia, He's going to empower us with fresh anointing to set things right again.

> *Those who think they can do it on their own end up obsessed with measuring their own moral muscle*

but never get around to exercising it in real life.
Those who trust God's action in them find that
God's Spirit is in them—living and breathing God!
(Romans 8:5)

Pentecost comes to fill us afresh with a living, breathing God. In a more manifest way, God's life becomes experientially real.

For you who welcome him, in whom he dwells...you
yourself experience life on God's terms (Romans
8:10).

That's the focus of Pentecost. It's about filling us with Holy Spirit to experience life on God's terms. I don't know about you, but I'm ready for life on God's terms.

It stands to reason, doesn't it, that if the alive-
and-present God who raised Jesus from the dead
moves into your life, he'll do the same thing in you
that he did in Jesus, bringing you alive to himself?
When God lives and breathes in you (and he
does, as surely as he did in Jesus), you are deliv-
ered from that dead life. With his Spirit living in
you, your body will be as alive as Christ's! ...God's
Spirit beckons. There are things to do and places
to go! (Romans 8:11-14)

There are gates, doors, and opportunities we are to pass through to new places, inheritances, blessings, and harvests.

This resurrection life you received from God is
not a timid, grave-tending life. It's adventurously

expectant, greeting God with a childlike "What's next, Papa?" (Romans 8:15)

The new-era Pentecost outpouring concerns what comes next on Papa's timeline. Breakthrough is being birthed on this planet through the Ekklesia, and doors are opening into a greater era of intense glory.

> *God's Spirit touches our spirits and confirms who we really are. ...And we know we are going to get what's coming to us—an unbelievable inheritance! ...That's why I don't think there's any comparison between the present hard times and the coming good times. The created world itself can hardly wait for what's coming next* (Romans 8:16-19).

An unbelievable inheritance is coming to us. We're going to have confirmed to us more of who we really are and it's going to be good times, not bad. If God's Word says it is, then it is.

> *Everything in creation is being more or less held back. God reins it in until both creation and all the creatures are ready and can be released at the same moment into the glorious times ahead. Meanwhile, the joyful anticipation deepens. All around us we observe a pregnant creation. The difficult times of pain throughout the world are simply birth pangs. But it's not only around us; it's within us. The Spirit of God is arousing us within. We're also feeling the birth pangs. These sterile and barren bodies of ours are yearning*

for full deliverance. That is why waiting does not diminish us, any more than waiting diminishes a pregnant mother. We are enlarged in the waiting. We, of course, don't see what is enlarging us. But the longer we wait, the larger we become, and the more joyful our expectancy (Romans 8:20-25).

AN UNBELIEVABLE INHERITANCE IS COMING TO US.

We are being enlarged in the waiting and receiving insight for our times. Our dreams, concepts, visions, and prophetic words are being ripened, and it's breaking open doors for us to run through.

DECREES

1. WE DECREE every yoke of bondage is broken.
2. WE DECREE God is changing our times and our seasons.
3. WE DECREE a new Pentecost is anointing us for supernatural acceleration.
4. WE DECREE the fivefold ministry will now activate to equip the saints for ministry.
5. WE DECREE we are passing through gates to new blessings and harvest.
6. WE DECREE the birth of a new Kingdom of God movement on the earth.

7. WE DECREE Holy Spirit is bringing order into the disorder of this world.

8. WE DECREE unbelievable inheritance is coming to us.

9. WE DECREE the cure for deadness— resurrection.

10. WE DECREE break up, break out, break through, passover, and possess.

Chapter 4

PENTECOST AND DIVISIONS OF ANGELS

We are living in one of the most opportune and strategic times in Christian history. The days, as in the book of Acts, are upon us.

> *But you shall receive power (ability, efficiency, and might) when the Holy Spirit has come upon you, and you shall be My witnesses in Jerusalem and all Judea and Samaria and to the ends (the very bounds) of the earth* (Acts 1:8 AMPC).

We are moving by divine plan into a mega-Pentecost outpouring of the Holy Spirit. This will activate and release supernatural anointing for God's people to prevail. It will also release many of the promises for which the true church has been believing. This will be true both corporately and individually. This mega-Pentecost will activate the release of millions of angels that have been filling their positions in multiple divisions under Holy Spirit supervision and alongside angel princes such as Michael, Gabriel, and other angel generals.

There are millions of angels in each division. The apostle John, in the book of Revelation, said they are innumerable. We are moving into the era when more angels will be sent from Heaven to assist Christ's heirs than any other period in history.

This is why Holy Spirit has been revealing the divisions of angel armies to me. It's time to engage with them as Holy Spirit leads. It's time for the assistance of angels partnering with Christ's Ekklesia, His New Testament church, at levels never before seen. The apostle Paul tells the Hebrews of angel assistance in Hebrews 1:14:

> *Are not all the angels ministering spirits sent out [by God] to serve* (accompany, protect) *those who will inherit salvation? [Of course they are!]* (Hebrews 1:14 AMP)

That's us. We are heirs. Heirs of God and joint heirs with Christ (see Rom. 8:17).

> *On the day of Pentecost all the believers were meeting together in one place. Suddenly, there was a sound from heaven like the roaring of a mighty windstorm, and it filled the house where they were sitting. Then, what looked like flames or tongues of fire appeared and settled on each of them. And everyone present was filled with the Holy Spirit and began speaking in other languages, as the Holy Spirit gave them this ability* (Acts 2:1-4 NLT).

At the beginning of 2020, Holy Spirit spoke to me concerning a new-era decade of greater glory and a special Pentecost that was now fully come. It was in its fullness of time. He specifically stated, "My people will move into a new-era Pentecost." I thought about that for days. What is a new-era of Pentecost? I knew it was something different than any of the other Pentecosts throughout history.

He then said:

> This year, the Ekklesia leaves its training and begins deployment. This will be a year of deployment and change for your future. The functioning Ekklesia will now rise to operate in higher authority and its advance will be rapid. The world will see the deployment of Heaven's Kingdom Ekklesia and angel armies. They will be suddenly and aggressively revealed. The strongholds of hell will be broken by the deployment, and iniquitous roots will wither under its superior power, authority, and administered justice. The withering of hell's kingdom will begin to be seen in indisputable ways, for the heirs of Kingdom authority will be seated in their regional spheres of influence. Their angels are aligning with the assigning, and you will now see a clear merger of Heaven and earth in unified oneness of purpose to escalate the King's victories, expand His Kingdom throughout the earth, and implement His Kingdom government. The merger of earth realm with spirit realm will surge in this new Pentecost era.

The word *new* was emphasized. After Holy Spirit spoke, I began to feel a vibration in my spirit. It was as if my spirit resonated with the promise of a new Pentecost. Not just another

Pentecost, but something new would be implemented. There are three literal Pentecosts that are important to understand in order to discern our times. Pentecost occurs every year and has been celebrated ever since the Exodus. They are feasts of remembrance and thanksgiving that commemorate what occurred at the first Pentecost.

The first literal Pentecost took place 50 days after the first Passover. Moses led God's people to Mount Sinai, and they camped around the mountain as Moses climbed up it to talk with God. During his time with the Lord, Moses was given God's Word, God's laws, and the Ten Commandments, and the Torah (the first five books of the Bible) began to be downloaded.

The Israelites celebrated this with a feast called Shavuot (or Feast of Firstfruits), which the Greeks called Pentecost. They celebrated God giving them harvest by bringing Him a firstfruits offering, or the first part of their harvest. Shavuot also celebrated God revealing His Word, laws, and commandments to them.

The second literal Pentecost took place in Acts 2, 50 days after Jesus became our Passover Lamb on the cross, when Holy Spirit was poured out on the 120 who had gathered in the upper room. He came to live in believers and to fill them with power from on high so they could be Christ's witnesses. He came to anoint them with a yoke-destroying anointing, to activate supernatural gifts, and to bear His supernatural fruit. He also came to birth Christ's church, Christ's Kingdom, and to establish apostles, prophets, pastors, teachers, and evangelists to equip the saints to do Christ's ministry.

Holy Spirit actually came. It wasn't just a celebration of ancient history. Power from Heaven was poured out and signs, wonders, miracles, and great harvest took place. The second literal Pentecost was magnificently "more" than the other Pentecosts of thanksgiving and remembrance over the past centuries. It was far more, as Holy Spirit actually came, and they were filled with His presence and power.

Holy Spirit is saying to the church today that we are now moving into a third literal Pentecost, far greater than Acts 2, with some new aspects added. This third Pentecost is activating the revelation of God's Word to, and through, His people in deeper ways. We will clearly see the plans and strategies that He will open to us in His Word. This new-era Pentecost will activate harvest, blessings, and power from Heaven. It is one that deploys the Ekklesia to function in higher authority and, merged with angel armies under Holy Spirit supervision, to disciple nations. This new-era Pentecost is surging in awesome glory and will overcome the kingdom of darkness, withering the roots and the fruit of hell with overwhelming power from Heaven. Please understand that this is not a one-time event but a continuous outpouring.

THIS NEW-ERA PENTECOST IS SURGING IN AWESOME GLORY AND WILL OVERCOME THE KINGDOM OF DARKNESS, WITHERING THE ROOTS AND THE FRUIT OF HELL WITH OVERWHELMING POWER FROM HEAVEN.

The angel armies are now being added in new ways, and at new levels, in this third literal Pentecost. The previous Pentecosts described angelic assistance, but now it will be far greater. Division after division of God's hosts, which have been reserved for our times, are being deployed with us. They partner to assist Christ's Kingdom government to break up, break out, break through, passover, and possess, just as they helped the Israelites break out of Egypt, passover, and possess their promise. And, just as they helped the people of God in the book of Acts break out of religious and government bondage, so they, too, will help us.

There is a Scripture that points to this in the Exodus. It's been overlooked, but it pictures an amazing promise of new Pentecost:

> Now the sojourning of the children of Israel, who dwelt in Egypt, was four hundred and thirty years. And it came to pass at the end of the four hundred and thirty years, even the selfsame day it came to pass, that all the hosts of the Lord went out from the land of Egypt (Exodus 12:40-41 KJV).

The word for *hosts* is the Hebrew word *tsebaah* and it means a large group of angels (Strong's H6635). It references the angel hosts, as in the hosts that surround the throne of God. It also references army troops, as in a large division of warriors, and it is the word for angel armies.

A host of people left Egypt with Moses, but so did the heavenly hosts that were assisting His people. It is both the people *and* the angels, and that's why it's worded this way. It's why this verse doesn't just say the people of God left Egypt. When you think about it, why would the angel armies stay? What would be the purpose?

The angels had been assisting and protecting God's people and helping Lord Sabaoth, the Lord of angel armies, release plagues so His people could be free. The angels of the Lord, who were assisting the Israelites to take great wealth out of Egypt, were no longer needed in Egypt. Their assignment had been to assist God's people to break out of 430 years of bondage. Now, God has led the people out of that bondage, and the angelic hosts serving that God-ordained purpose left as well. The angel armies went along with the people to protect them, to help with provisions, and to one day in the future help Almighty God break them into new lands of promise. This would begin with an amazing breakthrough at Jericho, where the walls were so thick, horse-drawn chariots could ride and patrol on the top of them. Those walls were busted, shattered, and broken up by God's breakthrough angels, and God's people entered supernatural breakthrough.

> *The people of Israel had lived in Egypt for 430 years. In fact, it was on the last day of the 430th year that all the Lord's forces left the land* (Exodus 12:40-41 NLT).

Please note the wording—*all* the forces of the Lord left the land.

> *The Israelites had lived in Egypt 430 years. At the end of the 430 years, to the very day, God's entire army left Egypt. God kept watch all night,*

watching over the Israelites as he brought them out of Egypt (Exodus 12:40-41).

Notice again: God's *entire army* left Egypt with His people.

In the book of Acts, when Pentecost was fully come, Holy Spirit came to baptize God's people with power from on high. He also brought angel armies with Him. They are seen as tongues of fire hovering over the 120 gathered in the upper room. Angels often appear in God's Word as flames of fire, as I wrote in my first book, *Angel Armies.* They came to assist the Kingdom of Heaven to break out, and to assist the apostles and the prophets in the first Ekklesia in breaking open a move of God on the earth, helping to expand the newly born Kingdom of Jesus Christ.

The angels accomplished this through Holy Spirit empowerment and guidance. Now, the promise of the Lord is that it's time for another literal Pentecost. Holy Spirit is coming to pour out power from Heaven. He's coming to pour out an anointing to prevail. Just as the precedent reveals in the previous Pentecosts, He is coming with the hosts of Heaven, bringing angel armies with Him in far greater measure.

The division of breakthrough angels will accompany Him to assist us in breaking out into the greatest move of God on the planet. Also, angels of awakening, revival, healings and miracles, deliverance, communication, enlightening, and war are coming with Him.

He promised this literal Pentecost, which is far more than just a single day, would begin an era of outpouring after outpouring, replenishing outpourings. He promised that He was bringing division after division of angel armies to the battle lines to assist our breakthroughs and victories.

This third literal Pentecost is different from the others, which were more localized. The first Pentecost in Exodus targeted one nation—Israel. The second Pentecost, in Acts, came upon a local New Testament church in Jerusalem—a rather small group of 120 people—though their affect grew in gigantic ways, turning the world upside down. Other outpourings from then on were also mostly localized. For example, the revival in Wales spilled over to other regions, but it specifically targeted Wales. We have had great outpourings in our times in Brownsville, Florida and in Toronto, Canada and in a few other places, but it was an outpouring in those particular places, with people traveling from everywhere to experience them.

There are no longer just 120 of God's people in one church or one town (Jerusalem). There is not just one apostolic hub for power from Heaven to pour upon. There are not just 11 apostles. God's people are now all over the world, in nation after nation, by the millions. There are apostolic and prophetic hubs, or New Testament churches, all around the world by the multiplied hundreds of thousands.

Today's outpouring will not be localized to a particular nation or church. This one will be the first Kingdom-wide outpouring, which has never before happened. The outpouring of the book of Acts birthed the church and Christ's Kingdom, but that Kingdom was small and functioned locally, at least in its beginning. But now, it's global. Now, Ekklesias are decreeing God's Word into regions everywhere. Now, the heirs of God and joint heirs with Christ understand their authority.

By necessity, by the sheer number of saints and churches, this outpouring must be far greater, and it will be. The plan of God is to soak a Kingdom of Ekklesias with power from on high. His plan is to assist them with millions of angels, in multiple divisions, operating under Holy Spirit guidance. His plan is to overwhelm the forces of hell with a worldwide outpouring. Hell has never before faced anything like it.

This will activate a worldwide move of God that hell can't stop. Everywhere it attempts to advance, it will face an Ekklesia and its angel armies, empowered and led by Holy Spirit. This era of Pentecost outpourings will also activate Holy Ghost and fire, setting ablaze a worldwide revival—a billion-soul harvest, at the least—and angels are coming to help us reap it.

> He answered and said to them: "He who sows the good seed is the Son of Man. The field is the world, the good seeds are the sons of the kingdom, but the tares are the sons of the wicked one. The enemy who sowed them is the devil, the harvest is the end of the age, and **the reapers are the angels**" (Matthew 13:37-39 NKJV).

We are now leaving training time for reigning time.

DECREES

1. WE DECREE an innumerable number of angels are activating to assist us.
2. WE DECREE we are now leaving training time for reigning time.
3. WE DECREE the Ekklesia will now deploy.

4. WE DECREE power from Heaven is anointing us to see signs, wonders, miracles, and great harvest.

5. WE DECREE the roots of hell will wither and die.

6. WE DECREE the greatest surge of the Kingdom of God overcoming the kingdom of darkness.

7. WE DECREE His presence will surge and be manifestly real.

8. WE DECREE Holy Spirit empowerment and guidance.

9. WE DECREE Holy Spirit and His angels are delivering us from confinement.

10. WE DECREE break up, break out, break through, passover, and possess.

Chapter 5

CHARIOTS OF FIRE

In 2016, Prophet Chuck Pierce gave a word at The Oasis that caused me to dive in and study a principle for the body of Christ concerning angels. Here is that word:

> The Lord says My Ekklesia will now start a movement between Heaven and earth. It is that movement that will usher in the angels. I say I am sending commotion in so that commotion will begin to happen in this land. I say these angels that you will open the way for will start rearranging and creating chaos throughout the land. I say do not sit back and watch the chaos as it goes through the land. I say it will be as chaos comes in and is created that My people will be able to see the order being created out of the chaos. I say when you open this portal it will create a sound that starts a movement in this land that cannot be stopped. I say I will realign My people and they will be like a locomotive that is moving and they will begin to move in a way that cannot be stopped.

It begins when you open this portal. I say now the portal for the move of God will be opened in this land. Open the portals that ushers in the angels.

There is a man in your kingdom in whom is the Spirit of the Holy God. And in the days of your father, light and understanding and wisdom, like the wisdom of the gods, were found in him; and King Nebuchadnezzar your father—your father the king—made him chief of the magicians, astrologers, Chaldeans, and soothsayers. Inasmuch as an excellent spirit, knowledge, understanding, interpreting dreams, solving riddles, and explaining enigmas were found in this Daniel (Daniel 5:11-12 NKJV).

An excellent spirit, knowledge, and understanding to interpret dreams, clarify riddles, and solve knotty problems were found in this same Daniel (Daniel 5:12 AMPC).

There was no one quite like him. He could do anything—interpret dreams, solve mysteries, explain puzzles (Daniel 5:12).

Daniel, who was brilliant and on par with Moses and Solomon, is one of the foremost prophets we are still studying to this day. Daniel revealed several essential keys in how he lived and conducted his life that are vital to us for interpreting our own times.

To accurately interpret the era in which he lived, Daniel received insight and understanding through various means. He would study and pray through the meaning behind dreams, visions, and prophetic words. He also explained riddles, which are statements or questions intentionally phrased so as to require ingenuity in ascertaining the answer or meaning. Daniel could solve complex mysteries, which speaks to things that are hidden from the obvious, and he also interpreted angelic visitations and what those angels communicated to him.

Daniel accomplished all these things through Holy Spirit inspiration. Jesus said that Holy Spirit is our helper and teacher in John 14:26. One way in which Holy Spirit assists us is through angels. Hebrews 1:14 says, "Are they not all ministering spirits, sent forth to minister for them who shall be heirs of salvation?" (KJV). Angels and their workings occur throughout the book of Daniel. Daniel said that he saw mighty princes assisting God's people. In Daniel 7:10, he saw ten thousand times ten thousand (one hundred million) angels assisting Father God around the throne of Heaven.

We need to understand this, as it is instructive for our times. Thousands of angels had assisted the people of God in getting out of Babylonian captivity. It was not just the archangels, Michael and Gabriel, but also the angel armies they commanded who battled against the Prince of Persia—a demon prince—and his demon armies. They were battling in the spirit realm to open up some doors for Daniel in the natural realm.

Daniel referred to some of the angels that he saw as "watchers." Daniel 4:13 and 4:17 tells us very clearly that the watchers were angels, holy ones from Heaven. These angels were sent by Holy Spirit to assist Daniel and the people of God who were in captivity. They were connecting to promises and answers to prayer, battling to open doors, and changing the hearts of kings and the government of his time. Specifically, these angels issued decisions on the earth and decreed a sentence of judgment against King Nebuchadnezzar that Daniel interpreted in a dream that he had.

Nebuchadnezzar would be banished from ruling as king for seven seasons. We don't know what the seasons were, whether it was for seven months or seven years. Many believe it referred to seven years, but at least for seven periods of time, Nebuchadnezzar would be removed as king of Babylon. The watchers, holy ones from Heaven—the angels—decreed that Nebuchadnezzar would lose his mind and would live like a wild animal, eating grass, sleeping in the wilderness, getting rained on, and being covered with dew. After the seven periods of time, he would once again be restored to the throne as king. This restoration would take place, the watchers said, after Nebuchadnezzar had learned his lesson to not blaspheme against God.

> *The angels announce this decree, the holy watchmen bring this sentence, so that everyone living will know that the High God rules human kingdoms. He arranges kingdom affairs however he wishes, and makes leaders out of losers* (Daniel 4:17).

These watchers/holy ones/angels helped Daniel and God's people see a rebellious government sentenced and changed. They saw Jehovah God proclaimed as the ultimate ruler over natural kingdoms. I believe that something very similar is now happening in the spirit and the natural earth realms today. Angels are going to help the King's Ekklesia pass sentence on rebellious governments and on doctrines of devils.

Daniel, of course, was an Old Testament prophet and he saw all of this angel activity. We are New Testament heirs of God, joint heirs with Christ, and have greater authority than Daniel ever thought about having. A part of our prophetic destiny involves the activation of millions of angels to assist us in this new era decade when the Ekklesia becomes the King's mouth. It's not a matter of just a few angels here and there. Rather, it is millions of angels with all kinds of different abilities, callings, and giftings that are watching from everywhere to assist us. They are here to help us activate prophetic destiny, if we will just search it out and find it. According to Psalm 103:20, they are here to hearken and help make happen the word of God that we, the Ekklesia, declare and decree in His Name. Revelation 5:11 tells us there is an innumerable number of them: "And I beheld, and I heard the voice of many angels round about the throne and the beasts and the elders: and the number of them was ten thousand times ten thousand, and thousands of thousands" (KJV).

King David was allowed to see into the spirit realm in Psalm 68:17, where he saw 20,000 war chariots of God being ridden by mighty, fierce, powerful angels that were empowered for battle just over Mount Sinai. Not over the world, just over Mount Sinai. It reads this way in the King James Version: "The chariots of God are twenty thousand, even thousands of angels." This number doesn't represent all the angels; there are plenty more of them besides these. I believe this chariot division is led by the angel Michael.

Second Kings 6:17 tells us that the prophet Elisha and his servant saw an innumerable number of angels in chariots of fire, and they also saw fire spirit horses. These were seen, not in the natural, but in the spirit, which doesn't make them any less real. In fact, the Scriptures teach that the spirit realm is *more* real than the natural realm, because the spirit realm is eternal while the natural realm is temporary. So please understand that the spirit horses and chariots were real. It was God's way, in Second Kings, of showing man that He has the most powerful army that there is, and it's real. He has a cavalry that's available to come to His people's aid, to fight for and with them, and to protect them. They are powerful enough to accomplish the mission against any activities of hell, or any activity in the natural realm, as when Elisha's servant had exclaimed that they were surrounded by the Syrian armies. When Elisha told him, "Don't worry...there are more on our side than on their side," the servant's eyes were opened and he saw God's awesome army.

Chariots and warriors were the measurement of a very strong army in biblical times, demonstrating the power and strength of a nation. Even now, horsepower is how we measure strength and power. If you purchase a car, they'll tell you how many horses are under the hood. They're not real horses, of course, but a representation of power, authority, and strength. Today, the Lord would perhaps use different descriptors, such as Abrams tanks, fighter jets, or hellfire missiles, to depict a powerful, mighty, overwhelming force.

We have powerful angels in God's cavalry division that are available to us and are now being emphasized by the Holy Spirit. The name of that division is not the Navy Seals, or the Army Rangers, or the Green Berets, elite warriors all. No, God calls His the "chariots of fire" division of Heaven's angel armies. For practical understanding, we could say that Holy Spirit is the Commander in Chief and Michael is the general of that division, as described in Revelation 12:7.

> *War broke out in Heaven. Michael and his Angels fought the Dragon. The Dragon and his Angels fought back, but were no match for Michael. They were cleared out of Heaven, not a sign of them left. The great Dragon—ancient Serpent, the one called Devil and Satan, the one who led the whole earth astray—thrown out, and all his Angels thrown out with him, thrown down to earth* (Revelation 12:7-9).

Lucifer led a coup d'état attempt against Father God in Heaven. He could probably have dealt with this several different ways, but the way He chose to deal with it is informative for us, His heirs. He asked Michael and his massive division of angels to deal with lucifer and the one-third of the rebellious angels who sided with him in battle against God. God said, "Michael, you and your angel army deal with this." Michael and his chariots of fire angels overwhelmed and overthrew lucifer and his angels.

This mighty division of angels is here today to assist the heirs and the Ekklesia of Christ Jesus. If God chose to use this division of angels, how much more important is it for us to be assisted by them as well. They are here and will hearken to the voice of our decrees made in the Name of King Jesus. This angel division has not stopped working; it worked with God in Heaven and it works with us on earth. There are simply times when, in spiritual conflict on earth, we must have the assistance of this mighty cavalry coming to our aid. It is available and one of the greatest benefits Holy Spirit is bringing to assist the glorious Ekklesia Jesus is building. This division has not died. There are no angel graveyards. They have not been retired. They are available as Holy Spirit leads, and we need to start getting the understanding of that spiritual dimension into our thinking.

I believe we are now moving into an era when angel armies, activated by Holy Spirit, will bring to pass the decrees of faith of the Ekklesia, helping bring to pass the strategies of Holy Spirit on the earth. The greatest decade ever planned by Holy Spirit is now unfolding before us and we're going to see more angel activity and more divisions of angels released to assist than in any other decade in all of church or world history.

The Ekklesia of King Jesus will experience the backing of Heaven's cavalry. They are here to assist God's heirs—the joint heirs with Christ—and they are going to do exactly that. Hell will find itself facing an awesome remnant warrior church army, and it will also find itself facing the chariots of fire that Heaven is activating on the earth. And, just as Elisha's servant saw, there are more of Heaven's elite warriors with us than those that are against us.

HELL WILL FIND ITSELF FACING AN AWESOME REMNANT WARRIOR CHURCH ARMY.

About seven years ago I had a reoccurring vision that I believe is connecting to its moment now. God has talked to me through visions since I was a small child. This particular vision I have seen many times since the original occurrence while praying concerning the purpose of God in our times.

The vision was of a long fuse, like the fuse on a stick of dynamite or a firecracker. I saw angels dressed like warriors (and I now believe they are a part of Michael's cavalry division) lighting these fuses. The fuses would begin to burn, spark, and sizzle like you see when a firecracker is lit.

But that's all I would see. I didn't see anything blow up! I didn't see any explosions, just the fuse was lit. And I didn't know what to make of it. All I knew was that the Lord was saying, "The fuse is lit," and I knew something was going to happen.

Seven weeks after I first saw the vision, Prophet Chuck Pierce came to speak at our Annual Prophetic Summit. At this summit he prophesied:

> The Lord says...there is an armory over you that I am preparing, and because of that the *dunamis* of

God will come alive and burst forth in this region. You will hear that a weapon has gone off and the Spirit of God has come alive and a weapon has gone off, and the Spirit of God has come alive, and all of the moves in the past will come together and look differently in this season. I say to you, I am forming a dome of glory over you and My people are becoming weapons in My hand. You will have armory meetings, saith the Lord. And in those meetings you will praise and the praises will cause you to be sharpened. A two-edged sword will come forth. I say to you, plan the armory meetings and a sound of glory will come. It will also be heard that riches and sources of income are being uncovered to resource you! I say to you, you are an armory for this nation. Prepare yourself and in the season ahead you will enter into the strategies that will war to save a nation. This nation will make its total shift. I say to you, let My armory form for this season.

We did, of course, begin those armory meetings. We call them "The HUB" and currently meet one Friday night a month. As you know, the hub connects the wheel for movement. We gather the Ekklesia from the region to worship, to hear the Word of the Lord, and pray for our nation.

I believe we are now in the season when all the moves from the past come together and nations will shift. It's not coming, it's here and we must step forward.

In the vision the fuse was lit by angels of war and I knew something was about to explode. The prophetic word is, "The *dunamis* of God will burst forth throughout the region." It will keep expanding and America will make its total shift.

I've been praying about this vision and this prophetic word off and on for seven years, and then we experienced a fresh, literal Pentecost in May of 2020. We knew Holy Spirit was bringing fresh *dunamis*. Since that time, I have been seeing this vision again but with more understanding prophetically. I began to see the angels lighting the fuses and fireworks exploding like you would see on the Fourth of July, but now they are exploding over apostolic and prophetic hubs all over the world.

I've been praying and pressing in and, of course, I've been asking, "Lord, talk to me, make it clear. Give me prophetic understanding." As I did that, I began to receive a download from Holy Spirit.

I heard the Lord say:

> You are moving into the explosive era of Holy Spirit power. My dunamis will activate and explosive energy will come upon My remnant. For I will now reintroduce Holy Spirit to the world.
>
> He will now be revealed in new ways to and through My people as the Mighty One of Heaven, filling My heirs with power.
>
> You are now entering the glorious season of Holy Spirit's explosive power that will be manifestly revealed. It will be seen. It will be felt. It will invade the earth, revealing the mightiness of the One who prevails.

For you have seen the incendiaries in the natural realm, now watch the incendiaries in the spirit realm. I'm bringing fire and activating dynamite. You are entering the time for the fire works of My Kingdom, says the Lord. (I heard the word *fireworks* as two words—*fire* and *works*.)

For you have seen the *fire works* of your adversary; now you will see Holy Spirit's *fire works*. You will see the fire power of My Ekklesia. It will not be fireworks of grandeur in the sky, streaking and falling to the earth for show. It will be the *fire works* of explosive power, raining upon thrones of iniquity.

My *fire works* will explode against demon princes. My fire power will explode, preparing the way for an invasion of My Kingdom and the establishing of beachheads where it had been forbidden.

My power will explode against rulers of darkness. They can scatter, they can run, but they can't hide. My warriors will find them and bind them.

I am coming to explode against and destroy the works of hell. This is not something I wish for; this is something I have planned for, says the Lord.

Holy Spirit has now released weapons of war that have been reserved for your times. New weapons are going off in the spirit realm. Hear the sound of the air raids.

Holy Spirit now declares, activate the air raids. Energize the word missiles. Empower the word bombs of the Ekklesia with dynamite. Fuel the word decrees of the King's Ekklesia with explosive power to demolish demonic blockades and establish new beachheads in the societies.

For as surely as fire rained on Sodom and Gomorrah, I will rain My fire on entrenched iniquity that has raised itself against Me. The combatives aligned with the forever loser who mocked Me will feel the explosive power of My might.

For this day I am releasing angels of war who will confuse the camps of My enemies. Watch, says the Lord of Hosts, as the enemies of My Kingdom begin to fight one another.

I decree friendly fire, friendly fire, friendly fire from the camps of darkness. I will divide their language and they will tear down their own evil towers. Watch, first will come the implosion. Yes, the battle against Me will collapse on itself. And then the spiritual explosions against the bases of demon strongholds.

I will not be mocked and I will not allow My heirs to be bullied. My power cannot be resisted and I will not relent. For I have heard the decrees of My faithful remnant who have executed what I say. Holy Spirit has filled their voice with *dunamis*. Decrees of faith will explode against strongholds. They will explode against schemes of evil. They will explode against garrisons hiding the enemies of My Kingdom.

I say the prevailing anointing of King Jesus, who always prevails, is now filling the heart and the mouth of My heirs. Bold determination is filling them. The warriors of My Kingdom will now march and activate, through Holy Spirit power, through baptisms of the Spirit of Truth Himself, word bombs from the glory dome against hell's kingdom, and earth's kingdom will shift.

Verbal missiles, launched under Holy Spirit command, will hit their mark. Verbal prophetic missiles, targeting Holy Spirit planned attacks in the spirit realm, targeting demonic princes, targeting the powers, targeting the rulers of darkness, targeting spiritual wickedness in high places. My word bombs will go off!

Angels directed by the Holy One have lit the fuses. I say now will be seen the foreordained plans of our special Pentecost. The season of Holy Spirit explosive power through the King's Ekklesia, the season when the angel warriors join forces with My heirs with explosive power, activated by Holy Spirit.

Supernatural power to reign will now manifest as My glory intensifies. Power that brought order to a mud ball will now be seen on earth as now Holy Spirit activates My power to bring order, alignment, and powerful displays of My creative abilities and the awesome displays of My constructive and reconstructive abilities to bring beauty from ashes. The oil of joy for mourning and garments of praise to displace the heaviness.

Holy Spirit will now reveal the determinant council of our will for the King's Ekklesia. We have prepared it, we have launched it, now we will empower it. We will release angels of fire and glory presence to finish Our plan. They will assist the flourishing finish.

Watch the *fire works* exploding now from apostolic hubs. Watch the *fire works* of prophetic networks. Watch the verbal missiles, launched from My Word, through the Ekklesia, hit their mark. Watch as Holy Spirit comes to the earth in new ways, activating power in greater measure than has ever been seen.

I say enter the season of increased *dunamis*. Enter the season of increased Kingdom energy. Enter the season of Kingdom *fire works*, says the Lord. Hallelujah.

ANGELS OF ENLIGHTENMENT, REVELATION, AND COMMUNICATION

In Zechariah 1 and 6, the prophet Zechariah also saw some of these spirit horses, chariots of fire, and angels. They were real, but they were in the spirit realm. He not only saw them, he also heard and talked to at least one of the angels. I believe these angels are under the archangel Gabriel and are called angels of enlightenment or revelation. They are messengers who communicate enlightenment to the people of God, especially to the Ekklesia and the apostolic hubs. Zechariah saw these angels going all over the earth, surveying it and its conditions (see Zech. 1:10-11). They were called "watchers" by both Daniel and Zechariah. In other words, the watchers observed and gathered information from around the universe for Holy Spirit and reported their findings back to the Kingdom of Heaven.

Angels of enlightenment, or revelation angels, explained matters to people in biblical times, such as Daniel, Abraham, Joshua, Jeremiah, Zechariah, Paul, Peter, and John, to name a few. These angels assisted Holy Spirit in downloading information to John in his book called the Revelation.

These highly trained angels are here right now, and in this new-era decade Holy Spirit is going to use them to activate revelation, enlightenment, instructions, and strategies, just as He did in the Old and New Testaments. They are going to be made available to us at higher levels, connecting the Ekklesia—the government Kingdom of God—to vital information that is beyond the natural realm of understanding.

As heirs, we have a right to special information that angels can connect us to. We have got to start opening up to spiritual resources that we have not yet been taking advantage of. We must come into agreement with Kingdom of God principles, or keys, and ask Holy Spirit to activate angels of enlightenment and revelation to come give us that information so we can function at a much higher and wiser level on this earth.

We have got to normalize what the nominal church and the world consider to be weird Christianity. We need to understand that true Christians and heirs are *supposed* to be assisted by angels. We're *supposed* to be guarded, delivered, strengthened, and connected to resources by them. Angels are *supposed* to assist in battle and set us free. We're *supposed* to be blessed and informed by them. It's in the Bible and we believe it.

It's time to raise the bar and stop living lowered, watered-down Christianity and begin living in Bible reality. Yes, angels assist me. Yes, angels sometimes talk to me and give me messages from Heaven. No, I am never alone. Holy Spirit is always with me and so are His angels. What's odd to me are people who see demons everywhere, hearing devils talking to them all the time. It's weird to listen to the devil and his demons. It's a whole lot smarter to listen to Holy Spirit and the real angels of God. Where in the world did we get so far gone that we think listening to angels is weird, and hearing from demons is *not* weird?

WE HAVE GOT TO NORMALIZE WHAT THE NOMINAL CHURCH AND THE WORLD CONSIDER TO BE WEIRD CHRISTIANITY.

Holy Spirit is saying, "I want you to pray and decree a portal to open over you, releasing the chariots of fire to ascend and descend in your base at a higher level. Decree the heavens open over you and welcome the cavalry of Heaven's mighty special forces to encamp round about you and to connect with the Ekklesia hubs. Invite them to base their work in your region, and empower them to work through decrees of authority and prayers of faith."

Obviously, this is going to help change the future. We need to declare the portal open for angels of enlightenment to ascend and descend and engage with us, connecting us to supernatural information and understanding, intelligence gathering that we can't do, and secrets, conditions, enemy tactics, and positioning that they are commissioned to communicate to us. This will accelerate a movement that cannot be stopped.

The prophet Zechariah also says in Zechariah 1 and 6 that these angels were some sort of reconnaissance soldiers, like heavenly scouts, for the Kingdom of God that were sent down from Holy Spirit. Zechariah tells us these angels rode powerful, energetic spirit war horses with distinct colors of red, black, dappled gray, chestnut, and white. These horses were galloping to patrol the whole earth, while the angels riding the horses and the angels in the chariots of fire were shouting, "On your way—survey the earth." These angels assessed conditions upon which Holy Spirit can implement strategies through God's people. We're starting to see how the Kingdom functions. Why does God do it that way? I don't know that we will know on this side of Heaven. We can only identify what is happening and we need to maintain our focus.

In Second Kings 2:11, the prophet Elijah saw the chariots of fire and mighty angels. I doubt he was singing the song that we often hear, "Swing low, sweet chariots." I don't think that there's anything sweet about them. It was time for Elijah to die and Elisha wanted his mantel—his ministry coat. Elijah had asked Elisha, "What's your request before I leave?" Elisha answered, "I want a double portion of the anointing that's on you. I want to be your successor." Elijah told him, "You're asking a hard thing, but if you see me when I go, the request is going to be granted to you." This story is one of the most fascinating accounts of the spirit and natural realms coming together in a visibly real way, which I believe is going to happen more frequently in this decade. We're going to see a manifestation of the spirit realm and the natural realms where the Ekklesia is concerned.

The story of Elijah and Elisha unfolds this way in Second Kings:

> *Just before God took Elijah to heaven in a whirlwind, Elijah and Elisha were on a walk out of Gilgal. Elijah said to Elisha, "Stay here. God has sent me on an errand to Bethel."*
>
> *Elisha said, "Not on your life! I'm not letting you out of my sight!" So they both went to Bethel.*
>
> *The guild of prophets at Bethel met Elisha and said, "Did you know that God is going to take your master away from you today?"*
>
> *"Yes," he said, "I know it. But keep it quiet."*
>
> *Then Elijah said to Elisha, "Stay here. God has sent me on an errand to Jericho."*
>
> *Elisha said, "Not on your life! I'm not letting you out of my sight!" So they both went to Jericho.*
>
> *The guild of prophets at Jericho came to Elisha and said, "Did you know that God is going to take your master away from you today?"*
>
> *"Yes," he said. "I know it, but keep it quiet."*
>
> *Then Elijah said to Elisha, "Stay here. God has sent me on an errand to Jordan."*

Elisha said, "Not on your life! I'm not letting you out of my sight!" And so the two of them went their way together.

Meanwhile, fifty men from the guild of prophets gathered some distance away while the two of them stood at the Jordan.

Elijah took his cloak, rolled it up, and hit the water with it. The river divided and the two men walked through on dry land.

When they reached the other side, Elijah said to Elisha, "What can I do for you before I'm taken from you? Ask anything."

Elisha said, "Your life repeated in my life. I want to be a holy man just like you."

"That's a hard one!" said Elijah. "But if you're watching when I'm taken from you, you'll get what you've asked for. But only if you're watching."

And so it happened. They were walking along and talking. Suddenly a chariot and horses of fire came between them and Elijah went up in a whirlwind to heaven. Elisha saw it all and shouted, "My father, my father! You—the chariot and cavalry of Israel!" When he could no longer see anything, he grabbed his robe and ripped it to pieces. Then he picked up Elijah's cloak—all that was left of Elijah!—and hit the river with it, saying, "Now where is the God of Elijah? Where is he?"

When he struck the water, the river divided and Elisha walked through.

The guild of prophets from Jericho saw the whole thing from where they were standing. They said, "The spirit of Elijah lives in Elisha!" They welcomed and honored him (2 Kings 2:1-15).

The cavalry angels that came to escort Elijah in a whirlwind did not pass away. They have not retired. The bronze chariots of fire have not been scrapped, nor have the war horses of Heaven been put to pasture outside the pearly gates. They are real, but unseen with our natural eyes. They are in spirit realms and are part of the King's cavalry. In this decade of the functioning Ekklesia, we are beginning to see the activation of chariots of fire once again.

THE BRONZE CHARIOTS OF FIRE HAVE NOT BEEN SCRAPPED, NOR HAVE THE WAR HORSES OF HEAVEN BEEN PUT TO PASTURE OUTSIDE THE PEARLY GATES.

When the Ekklesia becomes the King's mouth on earth, declaring what He says, forbidding what He says should be forbidden and permitting what He wants permitted, we are going to see the chariots of fire, mighty warriors of Heaven, come to our aid and defense. We will see the King's cavalry engage with us in ways that have not been seen for centuries. We are about to see the weapons of our warfare that have been reserved for an operational Ekklesia. Information will be revealed, enabling us to release decrees that need to be decreed. We have entered into the God-planned season of spiritual whirlwinds and chariots of fire in the hands of Heaven's warriors, coming to assist the transition of ministers and ministries and the promotion of servants. Indeed, apostolic chiefs are now rising and a division of angels called "Chariots of Fire" is going to back them.

Prophetic chiefs are also rising. These mighty angels of fire, this awesome spirit-realm cavalry, and especially the watchers, are going to battle hell's agenda for the release of prophetic decrees on the earth. We now have revelation and more access to information and understanding so we can make targeted decrees. Secrets are being revealed and, based on that, the Holy Spirit can begin to download it to the chiefs, and to the prophetic, and to His Ekklesia, in order to make the proper decrees. This will engage angel armies to operate with Holy Spirit.

Where is the God of Elijah? Where is the God of Abraham, Isaac, Jacob, Peter, James, John, and the apostle Paul? The world is about to find out where He is! He is in the midst of His glorious Ekklesia, just as He said He was going to be, making His stand with them. When He says He is going to have a glorious Ekklesia, He means it, and He is moving divisions of angels into place to assist. It is happening now and we have to discern what's going on.

Just as Elijah's servant thought, sometimes we think the numbers are too low. But not if you recognize there's a spirit realm with plenty of angelic warriors. As heirs of God and joint heirs with Christ, we are not helpless. We need to discern our times so we can function as Christ defined us. We have not done that yet, but we will, so we can operate in the real authority of the spiritual Kingdom of God, affecting the natural kingdoms of the earth.

Holy Spirit affirmed all these thoughts to me as I was watching a special documentary concerning the great war fighters of the United States who were helping to fight terrorism in Afghanistan. An Afghan general was interviewed and asked if he had a problem with our troops being on their base. He simply replied, "Oh no, not a problem at all. We welcome the greatest war fighters on the earth. We welcome them."

When he said that, I heard Holy Spirit say this to me: "You need to welcome the greatest cavalry to your base. You need to welcome the greatest war fighters, the greatest warriors in the universe, to your apostolic base. If you will, they will guard you from hell's terrorism and protect the awakening and the harvest of the ages that I have assigned to you." Please know we have awesome, fierce warriors available to share our apostolic and prophetic bases with us. We need to welcome them and release them with decrees of faith that Holy Spirit prompts inside of us.

We also need to welcome the division of angels under Gabriel—the angels of enlightenment, revelation, and communication—to be a part of our apostolic hubs. Under Holy Spirit supervision, these angels communicate special information, strategies and insight on the conditions of our world, and communicate the positioning of our adversaries in such a way that we can declare our freedom and live in the success our God intends.

Again, the name of this division is not Navy Seals, Army Rangers, or Green Berets, all of which are descriptive of awesome, elite warriors. God calls His division "Chariots of Fire," and as we move into this new era we will see the Ekklesia activate chariots of fire with their decrees as never before. Our assignments may be different, but chariots of fire are here to help. Let's activate the assignment of Heaven against hell's strategies. Our strategies will win. Hell's strategies will lose. We decree it in Jesus' Name.

DECREES

1. WE DECREE insight and revelation for our times is accelerating.

2. WE DECREE barrenness is broken and we are anointed to produce.

3. WE DECREE the watcher angels will communicate revelation and enlightenment to us.

4. WE DECREE God's cavalry will assist us to win great victories.

5. WE DECREE the portals open for angels to ascend and descend.

6. WE DECREE the chariots of fire are being activated by Holy Spirit to assist the Ekklesia and the new move of God.

7. WE DECREE the bar is raised and Holy Spirit is raising the anointing.

8. WE DECREE divisions of angel armies are based with, and work with, our apostolic hubs.

9. WE DECREE we are entering into God-planned seasons of spiritual whirlwinds.

10. WE DECREE break up, break out, break through, passover, and possess.

Chapter 6

GOVERNMENT ANGELS

Years ago when Holy Spirit began to download the revelation of angels and the greatest days in church history, I was in church on Sunday morning preparing to preach at The Oasis. As I approached the pulpit to deliver my message, I looked up toward the balcony and saw two massive angels. This was not a usual occurrence for me and it certainly wasn't something I was expecting. I hadn't prayed to see angels—they were just there. One angel was wearing a purple sash, while the other angel's sash was royal blue. At that time, I didn't know the meaning behind the different hues, but as soon as the service was over, I began to study prophetic colors and their prophetic significance.

In this chapter, we will discuss the purple-sashed angels, which are government angels. The color purple is associated with kings, royalty, and those who govern or rule. The millions of angels in this division are here to aid the Ekklesia in governing as intended and helping us to be a church that represents the Kingdom of God in a legal capacity. When an Ekklesia (a reigning church) makes a governing decree for a region, these are the angels that will pick up the decree and help to bring it to pass. They assist the Ekklesia in tearing down thrones of iniquity, which is deep-rooted sin, and they help the authority of the Ekklesia go to a different level in their region.

In the book of Daniel, Daniel had been praying over the future of his nation and had asked for help and wisdom from God. We are told that God heard Daniel's prayer the very first day that he started praying and had sent one of the most powerful angels, an archangel named Gabriel, with an answer. However, there was spiritual warfare that took place between Heaven and earth in the astrological, or atmospheric, Heaven between Gabriel and a demon prince, the spirit prince of Persia. This demon prince had sided with lucifer when he had attempted a coup in Heaven.

This spirit prince of Persia was warring against Gabriel to stop him from getting through to Daniel with the answer to the prayer. The battle lasted for 21 days and was quite intense. Here's what the Scripture says concerning Daniel's prayer and the ensuing struggle:

> *So listen, God, to this determined prayer of your servant. Have mercy on your ruined Sanctuary. Act out of who you are, not out of what we are. Turn your ears our way, God, and listen. Open your eyes and take a long look at our ruined city, this city named after you. We know that we don't deserve a hearing from you. Our appeal is to your compassion. This prayer is our last and only hope:*
>
> *"Master, listen to us!*

Master, forgive us!

Master, look at us and do something!

Master, don't put us off!

Your city and your people are named after you:

You have a stake in us!"

While I was pouring out my heart, baring my sins and the sins of my people Israel, praying my life out before my God, interceding for the holy mountain of my God—while I was absorbed in this praying, the humanlike Gabriel, the one I had seen in an earlier vision, approached me, flying in like a bird about the time of evening worship. He stood before me and said, "Daniel, I have come to make things plain to you" (Daniel 9:17-22).

Now, try to imagine this. You have prayed for 21 days, and after 21 days of spiritual warfare, Gabriel flies in like a human bird and says, "I'm here to help you. I'm here to answer your prayer."

"Relax, Daniel," he continued, "don't be afraid. From the moment you decided to humble yourself to receive understanding, your prayer was heard, and I set out to come to you. But I was waylaid by the angel-prince of the kingdom of Persia and was delayed for a good three weeks. But then Michael, one of the chief angel-princes, intervened to help me. I left him there with the prince of the kingdom of Persia. And now I'm here to help you

understand what will eventually happen to your people. The vision has to do with what's ahead" (Daniel 10:12-14).

Gabriel told Daniel, "I'm here to give you God's answer to your prayer and to help you understand the strategy of the King. You have a good future in store, and I'm going to assist you in understanding it." Clearly, God assigns angels to bring us answers to prayer. They organize around the prayers of the saints to bring them to pass—especially the prayers of an Ekklesia over a region.

I believe that's why the kingdom of hell fights corporate prayer so intensely. When the Ekklesia gathers in corporate prayer, it mobilizes angels. To change regions or to change a nation often requires angelic assistance, and it's why they have been given to us. Throughout Scripture, we see angels getting people out of trouble in their nations, cities, or in corporate ways, bringing answers to their prayers.

One of the ways in which you can identify whether you are in a brand-new era in the Kingdom is by fresh anointings of Holy Spirit. Everywhere I go, I am seeing new anointings and outpourings of the Holy Spirit. It's not like it was a few years ago; there's something happening in the atmosphere. Second, there is increased angel activity. Angels always assist the new eras and new moves of God. Study this in history and you will see angel activity every time. And third, the prophetic words of the apostles and the prophets will declare it. All three of those things are happening now in accelerated ways on the earth. I've never seen more Kingdom activity in my entire life; it's as if Heaven has amped up, and we need to amp up with it.

I want to describe something that happened in one of our church services that confirms that the Ekklesia's governing authority is now going to a different level, helping the church and prophetic words to connect to their moments.

I had just finished speaking on a Sunday morning at The Oasis and I felt that I should read several prophetic words at the end of the message. I have notebooks full of prophetic words from the past 20 years or so. I started to read one prophetic word after another from several well-known, leading prophets. Toward the end of my reading, the cloud of God's presence came into the room and I could only see those in the front row; I couldn't see anyone beyond them. This has happened several more times, where the cloud of God's presence has come in a tangible, real way. In three of our prayer assemblies around the region, the cloud of God's presence has come in and not left for days at a time. Another time, our praise team was traveling back on a bus from an assembly in Pittsburgh, and the pastor kept texting me that the cloud was still there. Their people began to send messages to other people, who started coming to that church to sit in the cloud of God's presence. This went on for three days. They took videos of the cloud hovering over where our praise team had stood. People would come up to worship and would walk into the cloud and not be seen until they walked back out of it.

As I was reading the prophetic words on that Sunday, the glory of God came in and angel activity starting occurring all over the room. I saw three groups of angels, with each group dressed in a different color. The first group was wearing purple sashes; the second group wore blue sashes; and there was a third group of bright, white light angels.

I knew this was a prophetic word of confirmation for the entire body of Christ for this new era, not just to The Oasis. After close to 11 years of studying angels and the prophetic meaning of their colors, I understood that the purple-sashed angels referenced government and that they were sent by the Holy Spirit to assist our Kingdom government, the Ekklesia, in governing things for the Kingdom of God on planet earth. Kings wear purple and fine linen. They are governors and they reign. Over the years, whenever I see government angels, I know something either needs to be forbidden or some kind of prayer decree needs to be made.

I remember when we went to Pontiac, Michigan and Prophet Chuck Pierce wanted to deal with the curse of Pontiac, the Indian Chief who, along with Tecumseh, had cursed the white man up and down the east coast. They had put a curse against our race because we had done some diabolical things to them, one of which was passing out scarlet fever blankets, which had nearly wiped them out. Chuck felt it was time to deal with the curse of Pontiac and to repent.

Apostle Barbara Yoder and I met up with Chuck at a hotel ballroom in Pontiac and the place was packed with intercessors. Chuck stood up and began to explain to the people why we were there. I was sitting in the front row, and as he spoke I saw government angels lined up behind him, all wearing a purple sash. I jumped up out of my seat, Chuck handed me the mic, and I said to the crowd, "The angels of God's government are here to assist our decrees. We can do this." The place just erupted into making decrees against Pontiac, repenting, and asking for the opening up of the East Coast for revival to begin to move up and down so that it could roll across the United States. As we made these decrees, the government angels left the building on assignment.

A few weeks later, we were doing an Appeal to Heaven Conference in Tucson, Arizona. I had preached on the Standing King in the evening, and the next day we were making prayer decrees. After I spoke, I stepped off to the side, and immediately I saw government angels with the purple sashes lined up all the way up one wall, across the back, and down the other side. I had never seen so many angels in one place before.

I said, "Holy Spirit, I've never seen so many government angels," and He replied, "There are 51 of them, if you want to count." I asked Him why they were here and He replied, "They are here representing each state capital and one for Washington, D.C. They're here to receive their assignments."

I told my brother, Dutch, what I had just seen and heard and we began making decrees. As the name of each state was spoken out, that state's angel would leave. Psalm 103:20 says when we decree the Word of the Lord, the angels listen. We kept praying and decreeing, especially over D.C., until all the angels had left the building.

The prophetic picture of this comes to us in the story of Esther and her uncle, Mordecai. Haman, a wicked government official, had tricked the king into signing an evil decree stating that anyone could kill any Jew that they wanted and confiscate their property. Unbeknownst to the king, Queen Esther and Mordecai were Jews. They went before the king and asked him, "Please, reverse this evil decree," but the king said, "No, I'm not going to do it. If you want the decree rewritten, you do it. I will give you authority to do it, but I won't do it for you." Esther 8 tells us the king then gave Mordecai his signet ring, which meant Mordecai could do business any time, any place, in the name of the king. It's like a corporate credit card, only better.

We are then told in Esther 8:15 that Mordecai's clothing was changed; they put different clothing on him in the king's presence. Most people have read right over this important sentence. The New King James says, "Mordecai went out from the presence of the king in royal apparel of blue and white, with a great crown of gold and a garment of fine linen and purple."

Mordecai left the king's presence dressed differently, in royal apparel of blue, white, and purple. Additionally, he received the king's signet ring and a crown of gold, which symbolized governing authority. Mordecai was mantled with the king's delegated authority to reign, govern, change laws, and make new laws.

Please hear what the Holy Spirit is saying about this new era: a fresh move of governing authority is now being given to the Ekklesia. Holy Spirit, the brilliant strategist, is releasing angels to assist that governing authority to come to pass. In this fresh move, angels will aid the saints in ruling and reigning on the earth at higher levels than have ever taken place in the Kingdom of God. Angels are assisting in opening doors for us:

- Doors to prophetic promises coming to pass;

- Doors to new miracles and the completion of long-awaited miracles;
- Doors to a new era for the saints to reign differently.

Just as Mordecai looked different when he came out from the king's presence, so the Ekklesia is going to look different in this new era. God is clothing us with governing apparel and a maturing of executive authority is going to be seen in believers everywhere. This precedent, seen in the first Ekklesia and in the first apostolic age, is happening now and it is being assisted by the division of government angels.

On May 18, 2019, I had a very unusual dream in which Attorney General William Barr was constantly being referred to as Mordecai Barr. An angel standing by my side said to me, "Mordecai Barr is hanging some government traitors." After he spoke, I heard a 21-gun salute like one would hear performed as an honor at a military funeral. In the dream, I was a little confused and questioned, "If it's a traitor being hung, why a 21-gun salute?" The angel replied, "That's not a 21-gun salute; that's a firing squad," and then I woke up.

I began to reflect on Haman, a government traitor in the book of Esther, who had built gallows on which to hang Mordecai. Of course, it was completely reversed and Haman was eventually hanged on the gallows he had intended for Mordecai. I believe this is an answer to the prayer decrees of the Ekklesia over the past several years. I believe it's a part of the exposing of corruption that God has assigned us to declare and decree, activating angels of chaos to tear off the band-aids and show the corruption. I'm of the opinion that this dream is a significant part of that deep state cleanup. I am not sure whether the 21-gun salute I heard in my dream was signifying that there were literally 21 traitors, but I believe God is assisting us to heal the land, using government angels and others to help us. It is part of our assignment, and we must pray for additional Mordecai Barrs to help complete this hanging.

A year after the dream, I was awakened on a Sunday morning with Holy Spirit speaking these words to me: "Press in with prayer and with faith decrees and birth the assignment on Mordecai Barr. It's connecting to its moment."

I believe God wants to give breakthrough to our nation. It's connecting to its moment; it's time. He is saying, "Church, you need to pray. Just as the prophet Elijah birthed the rain in prayer, you must birth this in prayer. Decree the breakthrough that I have promised you."

Something very big is up, and a shift in our nation can now occur. Though we may experience times of crises, we see all throughout the Word of God, and all throughout history, those are the times when breakthroughs begin to manifest. The true Ekklesia will rise up—not backing off—and what God says and has said will come to pass. If we will pray, He's going to guide our history right now and change its course. If we'll pray, we are going to triumph and win big, with the government angels of the Lord alongside us, assisting us in those prayers. Even diabolical laws that have contended against the Word of God can now be changed just like they changed in Esther and Mordecai's time.

On a recent Sunday morning, as I came into the church to pray for the upcoming service, I began to see a vision of a great shaking taking place in our nation and world. When I entered the sanctuary, I saw five government angels with the purple sashes, and I was caught up in the spirit and shown an earthquake. I saw this in the spirit realm, not the natural realm. I saw portions of the White House falling off and crashing to the ground under this severe shaking. I also saw portions of the capitol building in Washington, D.C. falling off, like you would see in video footage of the aftermath of an earthquake.

I then saw portions of all the states' capitol buildings, as well as universities, technology, giant businesses, and media, falling and crumbling as a result of the massive shaking. I watched as capitals of the nations around the world were falling. I could see the provinces in Canada crumbling under the intense shaking. There were national funerals with long lines, perhaps a mile or so, of black hearses. I didn't know if this represented people or the death of certain things, such as policies, laws, organizations, and ideologies. This was like a spiritual earthquake that was going to affect the entire world, and life was being taken out of something by this shaking. I heard Holy Spirit say these words to me as clearly as I've ever heard Him: "The shaking has begun."

The next Sunday, I was preparing to read the opening Scripture for that day's sermon when I heard Holy Spirit say, "The arrows of the Lord's deliverance have been released from the bow in Heaven." My mind flashed to the story of Elisha in Second Kings 13. Elisha was on his deathbed when King Joash came to visit him. Elisha told the king to bring him a bow and arrows. He then instructed King Joash to place his hands on the bow. When Joash did this, Elisha placed his own hands over the king's hands. To do this, Elisha would have had to get up from his deathbed to stand behind Joash. In this position, Elisha could then reach around and place his left hand over Joash's left hand on the bow and his right hand over Joash's right hand on the bowstring. Then Elisha told the king to open the window toward the east and shoot the arrow toward Syria, which he did. When the arrow was shot, Elisha prophesied, "The arrow of the Lord's deliverance," and he told King Joash that he must strike the Syrians until they were destroyed.

This was a picture of the apostolic and prophetic hand in hand with government authority in their nation. In our times, it pictures the true remnant warrior Ekklesia, based on the foundation of the apostles and prophets, also hand in hand with government authority. The phrase, "the arrow of the Lord's deliverance," references God striking His enemies, and the enemies of His people, with power that He activates through the apostolic, the prophetic, and His governing authority through the remnant, His Ekklesia. Holy Spirit was saying to me what He had said through the prophet Elisha, "The arrow of the Lord's deliverance has been released from Heaven."

I began to lead the congregation in declaring, "The arrows of the Lord's deliverance will hit the mark. The arrows will target the enemies of the Lord. The arrows will strike the enemies of God's Kingdom and bring mighty deliverance. The decrees of faith of the prophets, the apostles, and the Ekklesia will strike the mark. They will not miss. Great deliverance is now in our hands."

Since that morning, there have been striking blows to the deep state, to the CIA, and to the IRS. Striking blows have been delivered against political evils. Anti-Christ agendas against the church have been exposed, as well as a coup d'état against the President of the United States. Corrupt media agencies have been struck a blow that has devastated their influence, with several major news outlets facing bankruptcy.

A striking blow has also come against universities and their corruptions. It's been amazing the misuse of power that's being uncovered in nation after nation. The shaking has begun, the arrows of the Lord's deliverance have been shot, and God is cleaning house.

THE ARROWS OF THE LORD'S DELIVERANCE HAVE BEEN SHOT, AND GOD IS CLEANING HOUSE.

As I prayed about this, I recalled a portion of the prophetic word I had given in 2011 at one of our prophetic summits concerning a remnant that was willing to press in and pray for a Third Great Awakening. It was about becoming a true Ekklesia—a true reigning church—moving in Christ's authority and dealing with religious demons that stand in the way of the church, like Jezebel, Absalom, and present-day Pharisees, and it was about revival. I knew there was something in that word that was connecting to its moment. Here is a portion of that word:

> Great revival fire will burn throughout the world as My greatest awakening begins to move. Regions

and entire nations will become activated in My increasing glory. My shaking will come.

Walls, strongholds, obstacles of hell's fortification are being shaken down, even as you are being shaken free.

My shakings will open ancient wells of revival. I will shake open the capped wells of evangelism. I will shake open the ancient wells of healings, miracles, and mighty deliverance. I will shake down the barricades to new roads.

The Lord of Hosts decrees new roads, new inroads, new mantles, new vision, and new harvest! Behold, I do new things and you shall know it and see it springing forth.

Because your cries have come up before Me and because your worship has pursued My presence, the head of the church declares over His triumphant remnant: you will now begin reality church. No more acting, no more pretending, no more actors. Real church, real disciples, real Christians, real worshipers. Flowing in real glory, real power, real miracles, real healings.

It is ordained—reality church.

The Lord said I am removing the arrows shot in My ministers of righteousness. Arrows of betrayal, arrows from Jezebel, arrows from Absalom, arrows of deceit and gossip born in lying spirits, arrows by those bound by religious demons. I am removing arrows. You will be free. You will be healed. You will be restored and on fire with My presence.

For I have said, I will make My ministers a flame of fire. It is ordained, your place of pain will become the place you reign. Rise and rule with Me. I am now coming to My remnant as Lord Sabaoth, the Lord of Angel Armies, and for those who align with My purpose, I will now align My hosts to assist.

Battle lines are drawn. Strategies are in place. Preparations have been made. I will now gather My angel armies with My Ekklesia armies in a unified coalition. The coalition of My willing—those who run to battle, not from it.

My earth and My Heaven army will challenge thrones of iniquity, thrones of idolatry, thrones of rebellion, thrones of witchcraft, humanism, and anti-Christ demons. Entire divisions of angels are dispatched and await the decree of My words through My heirs. My greatest campaign is due; decree it. Align your words with Mine and angel forces will align with you. Align with the angel fires and it will accelerate an alignment of My purpose in the nations. Yes, revival is now. The harvest is now. The victory is now. Arise and pursue. Arise and roar. Arise and fight. Arise and shine, your light has come and the glory of the Lord has risen upon you.

The shaking has begun. Revival wells are shaking open. Harvests are being shaken free. Signs, wonders, and miracles are shaking free. Breakthroughs are breaking out. A divine shake-up is happening to shake us free.

Government angels are assisting the decrees of the Ekklesia to bring about the government of the Kingdom of God on the earth.

DECREES

1. WE DECREE the government angels are assisting the Ekklesia to reign with Christ.

2. WE DECREE demon princes over our regions are bound, in Jesus' Name.

3. WE DECREE the angels of the Lord are bringing our prayers to pass.

4. WE DECREE God's glory cloud will be revealed more and more over His Ekklesias.

5. WE DECREE doors to prophetic promises, new miracles, and the completion of long-awaited miracles done, in Jesus' Name.

6. WE DECREE the Ekklesia is being mantled with greater governing apparel.

7. WE DECREE the arrow of the Lord's deliverance in our times will hit the mark.

8. WE DECREE the shakings of our time will only shake us free.

9. WE DECREE this will be an era of reality church.

10. WE DECREE break up, break out, break through, passover, and possess.

Jackie 2/1/2021 (MON)

Chapter 7

ANGELS OF AWAKENING

In the previous chapter, I stated that I saw two angels in the balcony—one with a purple sash and the other with a blue sash. The color blue in Scripture represents revival, anointings, movings, and giftings of the Holy Spirit. In my study on angels, I began to understand that there are millions of awakening angels that are here to assist a new outpouring of Holy Spirit. I believe these are some of the same angels that were mentioned assisting Holy Spirit in Acts 2. There are no angel graveyards; angels don't die. They are still here, partnering with Holy Spirit in new moves, or campaigns, on the earth. They are here to release new anointings, one of which is the Standing King anointing that first occurred in Acts 2 when the Messiah was anointed as King of Kings and Lord of Lords. Our Father poured the anointing oil upon Jesus, which flowed down over His head until every part of His body dripped oil onto the people who had gathered in the Upper Room. Psalm 133 gives insight to bring this into the present. A part of that anointing is going to be released in our times. A portion of every outpouring down through history has been reserved for now.

THERE ARE NO ANGEL GRAVEYARDS; ANGELS DON'T DIE.

As I was praying and preparing for service one Sunday, I began to feel a prophetic anointing stirring inside of me. I continued praying in the spirit for another 20 minutes or so, when Holy Spirit began showing me a vision. Ever since I was a small child, God has shown me visions and then talked to me about their meaning. It's the foremost way in which He speaks to me.

In this vision, I saw a huge funnel, like the type that's used to pour oil into a car's engine, with a big bowl at one end and a stem at the other end. The bowl of the funnel was actually like a television screen and I began to see various scenes scrolling around the sides of it. There were scenes, one after another, of events down through the ages, including the book of Acts, church history and events, great revivals and prayer meetings, revivalists and evangelists, and other great movements of history. It was as if I was watching a movie. After a while, the scenes began to circle further down into the funnel bowl and were being squeezed into the narrow stem at the bottom, running out into our times.

Not wanting to surmise the meaning, I asked, "Holy Spirit, what are You showing me?" He answered, "I'm pouring the anointings and the streams of Christ's Kingdom throughout the ages into the new era we've prepared for the glorious

Ekklesia." I then asked, "What am I to do with this?" He stated, "You are to declare that it is now connected to its moment. The synergy and convergence of the ages have begun. The anointings and outpourings have begun. The activation of prophetic words has begun. Pray it, decree it, prophesy it, guard it. Steward its activation into your times."

His words then became like a prophecy: "For you have entered a fullness of time and are entering the second apostolic age, an era of signs, wonders and miracles." This was the second time Holy Spirit talked to me about the second apostolic age. "It is the era," said the Lord, "when the Ekklesia sits on the throne of their regions and influences the natural realms of earth through the spiritual Kingdom. Watch the Ekklesia rise, for it shall surely rise. It is purposed. It shall be so. It will rise and it will rule as intended, for it has now connected to its moment. Watch the change and the changes. Align with Heaven and you will see it on earth. Align with Heaven and activate the rapid change. Speak your agreement. Speak to the fog. Command it to lift and you will see the new era."

Recently, we received another dream from Gina Gholston. Gina had this dream when we were at the Trump Hotel in Washington, D.C. for the Appeal to Heaven Conference, the year after Trump was elected President. This dream had been read at that conference:

> I saw a mighty angel with a scroll and he began to walk throughout D.C. and over to Capitol Hill. He walked into the capitol and was in the place where the head usher walks into the House of Representatives

> to announce the President of the United States
> for the State of the Union address. Instead of the
> usher, however, the angel walked in, rolled out the
> scroll, and began to boldly announce, "Mr. Speaker,
> America shall be saved."

We received another significant prophetic dream from
Gina, which began like this:

> I dreamed I was on the grounds of the Red River
> Meeting House in Russellville, Kentucky.

Let's stop and talk about why this is important. It's
because the Red River Meeting House is where the Second
Great Awakening began in June of 1800. It's the first place
in America that ever had camp meetings. People came from
everywhere and the power of God would come upon them as
they took communion. They would sing, jump up and down,
leap, and dance. Some were overcome with the power of Holy
Spirit and would just fall to the ground. Someone remarked
that it looked as if Holy Spirit slew them, and that description
is still used today to describe being "slain in the Spirit."

The dream continues:

> I had gone through the gate and started walking up
> the driveway toward the Meeting House. In front of
> me, in the dip as you go up to the building, I noticed
> that there were close to 100 bald eagles standing
> on the ground. I was captivated by the sight of all
> the eagles.

I, too, have been captivated by eagles and have been studying them for over 40 years, so this grabbed my attention. I taught on *war eagles* after receiving a prophetic word on them, and that message has gone around the world. War eagles speak to an awakening in the coming generation, as we'll see in a later chapter.

The dream continues:

> Then, hearing a noise behind me, I turned and saw one of those older well drilling rigs coming through the gate toward the meeting house. It stopped about halfway up the driveway and backed up toward the meeting house, stopping under the walnut trees. Then, those on the truck began drilling, and no sooner had the bit been set when, whoosh—the water came gushing out in massive amounts. In the dream I thought, "This looks like Old Faithful." I have seen that geyser and this made me think of that, only this was much larger in the dream. I was thinking about how Old Faithful is very predictable and that it gushes forth in a rhythm of time. Then, I heard an audible voice speaking about the geyser in front of me that was now gushing forth, and it said, "It is set on the rhythm of Heaven's time clock. It's time."
>
> In this dream I understood that statement to mean that it's blown before. A gushing move of the Holy Spirit has blown before, but it's set for another, greater gush this time. Next, I saw two hands come down and clap once. The clap made a very loud

sound, and when it came it was a signal to the eagles. When they heard the clap, the eagles rose up, hovering, ready to fly. They weren't scared by the noise of the clap or by the spraying of the water. They all just simultaneously rose up and calmly hovered.

When they started rising up, I saw that each eagle carried arrows in one talon and rolled up papers in the other talon. As they rose up, hovering, I heard the voice say, "Rapid eye movement. My seers are on the move. My watchers are on the move."

As soon as I heard those words, the eagles flew off in every direction, each heading purposefully in the direction they were sent, carrying out their own assignments. As they left the Red River Meeting House, they each flew through the gushing water, getting the water on them and carrying it with them. The water never dried off of them. Wherever they went as they flew, the water would fall off of them like a rain shower onto the dry ground they were flying over.

The water was still gushing and I, too, was soaked with it. I went into the Meeting House, which was set up like a command center. There were perhaps seven drafting tables set up, with architects sitting at them, drawing up blueprints or plans. People were coming in one right after the other, soaked in the water from the gusher. Each person would approach one of the architects who were drawing up the blueprints, who would then tear off a blueprint, roll it up, and hand to the person.

It's hard to explain, but immediately after rolling up one blueprint, the architects would quickly have another one drawn, which they would roll up and hand off to the next person in line. I was amazed at the speed of the architects in their work. They were drawing, rolling, and handing—this was happening over and over, very, very quickly.

Then I noticed there were pipes built into the walls of the Red River Meeting House going out in every direction: north, northeast, east, southeast, south, southwest, west, and northwest. When the people received those blueprints, the architects would point them in the direction of a certain pipe. They would get in that pipe and be sent where they needed to go with those blueprints, those plans.

In the dream, I thought this process was similar to sending emails. I thought of fiber optics. I knew that, just like it was with an email, these people were getting into the pipes and were being sent along with the blueprints, strategies, plans, and revelations. Wherever in the world they were sent, as soon as they got in the pipe, whoosh—they instantly arrived at their destination, soaked with the water that had sprayed on them from the gushing well, raining off of them like it did with the eagles.

I then heard the same voice say, "Rapid response centers." I looked up on the wall behind the pulpit in the meeting house and I saw a sign that read, "Rapid Response Command Center." Then the dream

> shifted, and suddenly I somehow knew that what was happening at the Red River Meeting House was also happening at Cane Ridge, Kentucky and at Azusa in California.

Why was Cane Ridge important? The Cane Ridge Revival happened in 1801, a year after Red River. They had multiple communion services at that revival, and many preachers were there. People came from everywhere in carriages; there were no cars at that time. They brought their own food and would camp for days. Preachers would gather around the hillsides, one preaching here, another there, while another would find a tree and start preaching. They would draw the people in with a song and the preaching would begin, with sometimes two dozen preachers speaking at a time. They would have nightly communion and, on the weekends, they often had crowds of over 25,000 for communion. Cane Ridge, which is about 20 miles from Lexington, was one of the most amazing revivals that we have had in all of history.

The Azusa Street Revival occurred in 1906 in Los Angeles, California, led by William Seymour. This was the first time that many began to speak in other tongues. They were baptized in the Holy Ghost and held their prayer meetings in a local house at 216 Bonnie Brae Street. Later on, they would meet in a building on Azusa Street. They would get as many prayer warriors as they could into the house and begin to pray. One time, they prayed for three days, and people would try to get to the meeting, or even just pass by, and as they did they were slain in the Spirit in yards all around for almost half a mile. The power of God was beginning to flow.

Gina's dream continues:

> I was then lifted up and could see a drawing of a line connecting Cane Ridge, Kentucky and the Red River Meeting House, and going out from Cane Ridge were other lines, with one line from each of them going to Azusa. As I was lifted up high above the nation, I saw that these lines formed the shape of a spearhead. From the line that was drawn between Cane Ridge and Red River was another line and I knew that this line was coming from the nation of Wales.

This references the Welsh Revival that was led by Evan Roberts, which lasted from 1904 until early 1906. Over 150,000 people were saved in one year's time in the largest revival Wales has ever seen.

Gina's dream continues:

> It was a drawing depicting that all four of these places—Cane Ridge, Red River Meeting House, Azusa, and Wales—were all connecting, and that what I saw happening at Red River was simultaneously happening in all the other places. I knew I was being shown that the culmination of all those past moves of God were now being brought together to spearhead another greater and more powerful move of God in our times. They were converging.

Gina's thoughts concerning the dream:

> After I had this dream, I happened to find a page where I had transcribed a prophetic word that God had released to our region through Apostle Tim Sheets in August of 2019, while speaking at the Fire on the River Conference in Clarksville, Tennessee.
>
> God said through Apostle Tim, "I am sending My angels and they are preparing the ground for breakthrough. They are opening up the wells that I have placed in your region that have been capped by the enemy and capped by religious demons. But they are peeling back the layers and they are opening up those old wells and those wells will now spring up and you will move into the spheres of influence that I have purposed for you."
>
> Holy Spirit says the water from past moves of the Spirit of God is still available. Breakthroughs have come; wells have been uncapped. Now it is time for the gusher. It will happen at a rapid pace. It is set to the rhythm of Heaven's time clock, and it's time.

Hear what Holy Spirit is saying: "It's time for the gusher! It's time for old healing wells and revival wells to be uncapped. Awakening angels are connecting us to Holy Spirit strategies with past streams of revival and past anointings that are now activating in our times." New streams for our times are flowing and new anointings are synergizing together. It is time to see all of this; it's time for our future to change. A move of God is beginning that cannot be stopped.

The Welsh Revival that Gina saw in her dream speaks to me and I've been drawn to it for years. Several years ago, Carol and I drove up to Canada to minister at a conference. We arrived late in the afternoon and only had a little bit of time to freshen up at the hotel before being picked up to go to the meeting place. I was ready to go and waiting for Carol and only had enough time to ask, "Holy Spirit, why am I here? What are You saying?" Immediately the Lord spoke these words to me: "The revival in Canada will be like the Welsh Revival led by Evan Roberts." I wrote those words down, someone picked us up, and off we went to the meeting.

When we arrived, we stepped through the back door of an old hockey arena that held around 500 people. We were led through the door, past the platform and pulpit, to seats in the front row. When we walked in, I saw that the leader of the meeting had placed an old wooden chair near the pulpit, which I thought was a little unusual, but I didn't mention it. As I met with the leader prior to starting the meeting, she said to me, "Do you see that chair? That's Evan Roberts' chair from the Welsh Revival." I nearly fell over because of what Holy Spirit had spoken to me back in the hotel. I reached for my Bible and handed her the paper that had the words I had written just an hour earlier: "The revival in Canada will be like the Welsh Revival led by Evan Roberts." I had no idea, had never been in that arena before, and I certainly didn't know they were going to have that chair there. But Holy Spirit did, and He knew it would start speaking to us. Holy Spirit is saying to us, "Remember the Welsh Revival. Pick up the mantle of the Welsh Revival." This prophetic understanding is not just for

Canada but also for the United States. Holy Spirit has repeatedly spoken to me that the revival in America will be like the Welsh Revival.

Evan Roberts was a young man who worked in the coal mines; he was also a blacksmith. Today, we would define him as a millennial. Roberts spent hours praying and reading his Bible, often all night long. He was the youth pastor at his church and also taught Sunday school. At the age of 26, after praying and seeking the Lord for days, he felt led to go to a missions conference led by Evangelist Seth Joshua. At the end of the meeting, the evangelist prayed a prayer and one particular line was, "Lord, bend us," which was a phrase used in those times for holiness. It's not really used in that way today. In other words, "Bend us to follow You, Lord. Make our hearts pliable. Soften us, Lord. Bend us into who we need to be. Bend my life so it is usable, Lord. Shape us."

As Seth Joshua prayed, "Bend us, Lord," people in the congregation began to spontaneously pray out loud. Evan Roberts writes of that moment:

> When others prayed I felt a living force come into my bosom. It held my breath, and my legs shivered. ...The living force grew and grew, and I was almost bursting. ...I cried, "Bend me! Bend me! Bend us!" What bent me was God commending His Love...and I wept. Henceforth the salvation of souls became the burden of my heart. From that time I was on fire with a desire to go through all Wales.[1]

And the young man did just that. Conservative estimates are that over 150,000 gave their hearts to Christ. Bars closed and crime was practically nonexistent. The police actually said they had little to do besides managing the crowds who were going to a revival or church meeting. The people were so joyful, and they sang so much that the revival simply became known as the "Singing Revival."

Thousands of coal miners were saved, many of whom were hardcore sinners. These coal miners now loved to sing while they worked. It was said the mules that carted off the coal had to be retrained because they had been trained by these hard miners to follow the command of curse words; they didn't understand kind words.

The coal mine had large air shafts running hundreds of feet down into the earth all over the Welsh hillsides. People would bring chairs and sit around those air shafts, listening for hours to the reverberating songs and hymns echoing up from the bowels of the earth, from men who were now saved. The songs would travel down the line as various men joined in, singing for so long that all around the hillside you could hear the songs coming up from the earth. No one sings quite like the Welsh; theirs is an accent that gets into your soul. It is so hard to imagine this, but the countryside literally echoed with praise and worship wafting up from the ground. All of Wales was changed, and then the nations around them began to change.

The Welsh Revival connected to Red River, Cane Ridge, and Azusa, and now God wants to add it to our times. Music is going to be a vital part of this revival. The most notable song from the Welsh Revival is called "Here Is Love" and was sung hundreds and hundreds of times, with untold numbers giving their lives to Christ during the singing of it. It was sung so often it became known as the love song of revival.

HERE IS LOVE[2]

Here is love, vast as the ocean,
Loving-kindness as the flood,
When the Prince of Life, our Ransom,
Shed for us His precious blood.
Who His love will not remember?
Who can cease to sing His praise?
He can never be forgotten,
Throughout heav'n's eternal days.
On the mount of crucifixion,
Fountains opened deep and wide;
Through the floodgates of God's mercy
Flowed a vast and gracious tide.
Grace and love, like mighty rivers,
Poured incessant from above,
And heav'n's peace and perfect justice
Kissed a guilty world in love.
Let me, all Thy love accepting,
Love Thee, ever all my days;
Let me seek Thy kingdom only,
And my life be to Thy praise;
Thou alone shalt be my glory,

Nothing in the world I see;
Thou hast cleansed and sanctified me,
Thou Thyself hast set me free.
In Thy truth Thou dost direct me
By Thy Spirit through Thy Word;
And Thy grace my need is meeting,
As I trust in Thee, my Lord.
Of Thy fullness Thou art pouring
Thy great love and pow'r on me,
Without measure, full and boundless,
Drawing out my heart to Thee.

Holy Spirit has released awakening angels to connect us to the anointings of previous revivals. They are also connecting us to the great awakening that is planned for our times. They are connecting us to prophetic words, visions, and dreams. The Third Great Awakening has begun.

DECREES

1. WE DECREE the synergy and convergence of the ages has begun.
2. WE DECREE America shall be saved.
3. WE DECREE the war eagles are rising.
4. WE DECREE it is time for the gusher.
5. WE DECREE the Ekklesia will rise and rule as intended.
6. WE DECREE the anointings on the Cane Ridge, Azusa Street, and the Welsh Revivals will now synergize into our times.

7. WE DECREE Heaven's time clock is setting our heart in rhythm with God's heart.

8. WE DECREE new songs of revival will now activate.

9. WE DECREE bend us, bend us, bend us.

10. WE DECREE break up, break out, break through, passover, and possess.

NOTES

1. Evan Roberts, "Evan Roberts Testimony: 1878-1951," The Revival Library, accessed July 10, 2020, http://revival-library.org/index.php/pensketches-menu/evangelical-revivalists/roberts-evan-his-own-testimony.

2. William Rees and William Williams, trans. by William Edwards, "Here Is Love" ("Dyma gariad fel y moroedd"), printed in *The Baptist Book of Praise* (Wales: Baptist Book of Praise Committee, 1900).

Chapter 8

ANGELS OF REVIVAL

God grabbed me. God's Spirit took me up and set me down in the middle of an open plain strewn with bones. He led me around and among them—a lot of bones! There were bones all over the plain— dry bones, bleached by the sun.

He said to me, "Son of man, can these bones live?"

I said, "Master God, only you know that."

He said to me, "Prophesy over these bones: 'Dry bones, listen to the Message of God!'"

God, the Master, told the dry bones, "Watch this: I'm bringing the breath of life to you and you'll come to life. I'll attach sinews to you, put meat on your bones, cover you with skin, and breathe life into you. You'll come alive and you'll realize that I am God!"

I prophesied just as I'd been commanded. As I prophesied, there was a sound and, oh, rustling! The bones moved and came together, bone to bone.

I kept watching. Sinews formed, then muscles on the bones, then skin stretched over them. But they had no breath in them.

He said to me, "Prophesy to the breath. Prophesy, son of man. Tell the breath, 'God, the Master, says, Come from the four winds. Come, breath. Breathe on these slain bodies. Breathe life!'"

So I prophesied, just as he commanded me. The breath entered them and they came alive! They stood up on their feet, a huge army.

Then God said to me, "Son of man, these bones are the whole house of Israel. Listen to what they're saying: 'Our bones are dried up, our hope is gone, there's nothing left of us.' Therefore, prophesy. Tell them, 'God, the Master, says: I'll dig up your graves and bring you out alive— O my people! Then I'll take you straight to the land of Israel. When I dig up graves and bring you out as my people, you'll realize that I am God. I'll breathe my life into you and you'll live. Then I'll lead you straight back to your land and you'll realize that I am God. I've said it and I'll do it. God's Decree'" (Ezekiel 37:1-14).

In this passage in Ezekiel, we see a prophetic vision and hear a prophetic word. A "new breath" is entering God's people and resurrection life will cause them to come together and stand as a great army. As I pondered this important prophetic vision, I began to hear, in the spirit realm, the sound of a rushing mighty wind. I heard it for hours; it was the sound of a rumbling, from deep within.

I've hunted for elk high in the Rocky Mountains and, on some occasions, I've witnessed the treetops bending and rustling as the wind picked up. I've heard the thundering begin to vibrate deep in the forest—a roaring type of sound, off in the distance, that became louder and louder as it approached. That's comparable to what I began to see and hear in the spirit realm as I meditated on this passage.

On the day of Pentecost in Acts 2, a small remnant of 120 believers sat in an upper room in Jerusalem. They must have heard a similar type of sound from Heaven as Holy Spirit came as a rushing mighty wind, filling the house in which they had gathered. Life burst forth and transformation came as God's breath blew upon them and resurrection surged into a hopeless, fearful body of people. Disciples, buried by difficult situations and loss, came alive. Widows, orphans, and the poor, who had been entombed in societal grief and governmental domination by the Roman Empire, were revived.

As I heard the rushing mighty wind, I discerned it was coming from Heaven upon the remnant warriors who have been making their stand for Christ. I thought of the song "Revival" by Robin Mark:

> *I can hear that thunder in the distance*
> *Like a train at the edge of town*
> *I can feel the brooding of Your Spirit*
> *Lay your burdens down, lay your burdens down.[1]*

I began to picture sails, as on a ship, rising into Holy Spirit winds. A knowing in my spirit came—winds were going to blow the church from the doldrums into fresh waters and new ports of blessing. Holy Spirit was bringing fresh breath to "life" His body; it would no longer be a disconnected skeleton. The graves would be opened and the church would come to life.

The world has pronounced the church as dead. A demon-orchestrated mindset through media, education, business, the arts, and politics has pronounced the efforts of God's people, and the church, as irrelevant. There has been an attempt to bury Christianity through humanistic, New Age demon doctrine. There's a vicious war going on against our values, but God is saying, "Prophesy to the bones and command them to live. Prophesy to the winds, to the breath. Come and breathe upon these slain and watch My resurrection life transform them and their situations. Prophesy, live again!"

In Ezekiel 37, God was saying, "Watch this: I'm bringing the breath of life to you and an army is standing forth. It is not a dead army; it's alive." I am hearing the sound of rattling as bones are coming together, as ligaments and muscles are being formed. I hear the sound of wind resuscitating, invigorating, and "life-ing" God's people. Christ is not returning for a dead bride, dead church, or a demoralized, frightened army. He's coming for a glorious church without spot or wrinkle, one that will begin to disciple nations.

There is a cure for deadness. It's called "resurrection" and our King has it mastered. I don't hear funeral dirges, as some are proclaiming. I'm not hearing the bugle playing taps. I hear the sound of reveille. I hear resurrection life being breathed from the throne room. Like Elijah, I hear the sound of an abundance of rain. A fresh outpouring of God's Holy Spirit is on the move. A trans-generational anointing is available and the most alive body of people in history is emerging. They will possess the mountains of society, and hell will not overcome them.

Our King, along with Holy Spirit and His strategies, assisted by millions of angels, is working now to breathe life into the true church. It is accelerating into a spectacular movement confirmed by signs, wonders, miracles, healings, breakthrough, and harvest. A billion-soul revival is coming and a Kingdom move of God, greater than most have ever thought possible, has begun.

After pondering this strategic prophetic word for our times, I entered into the most incredible months of revelation that I've ever experienced. There were times when I could see and hear things more clearly, in the spirit, than at any other time in my life. We must understand that spirit realms are very real. They are not imaginary, spooky, or weird. It is actually normal Christianity to be in tune with the spiritual realm. We are to be spiritually minded as well as a wise, naturally minded people.

On February 14, 2019, I began to see, in the spirit realm extremely strong winds blowing from the four corners of the earth. Remember Ezekiel had prophesied in Ezekiel 37:9: "Come from the four winds, O breath, and breathe upon these slain, that they may live" (KJV). The New Living Translation says, "Come, O breath, from the four winds! Breathe into these dead bodies so they may live again." The Contemporary English Version reads, "Blow from every direction."

The words *breath* and *spirit*, used interchangeably throughout the text, are translated from the Hebrew word *ruwach* (Strong's H7307). Holy Spirit is the *ruwach* of God. He's the Breath Spirit that entered the lifeless skeletons, causing them to come alive.

In my vision, Holy Spirit was blowing life from all directions and I could see thousands of angels riding upon those four winds. They looked to me like flying clouds of angels, just as thousands of birds look like in the winter when they flock together so densely that they look like a flying bird cloud. I began to pray, "God, what are You showing me? Give me understanding." In my spirit, I heard Holy Spirit say, "This is a division of angels now being released for the new days."

Over the next several days, I continued praying and asking, "Lord, who are they? Show me; what do they do?" At the end of five days, something happened to me that has never occurred before. On Monday, February 18, I began to hear and see one word, over and over, all week long. When I looked at signs, such as a billboard, this one word would appear on the sign. I could see the original words of the sign, but then those words would transform into this one word, almost as if it was superimposed over the initial words. The word was *revival*, but it was spelled differently. The word I saw was *re-vive-all*.

I began to see it everywhere. I would see a stop sign and re-vive-all would superimpose upon it. This happened repeatedly, with other signs. Also, in my spirit I heard the word re-vive-all echoing over and over. I even thought I heard it spoken out loud. During this time, Holy Spirit began to download information to me concerning this word signifying a division of angel armies. I knew that this was about the magnificent revival that has been prophesied for decades.

Re-vive-all angels are being deployed on Holy Spirit winds. They are being activated and are riding Breath Spirit's wind into all the earth. They are assisting Holy Spirit's strategy to re-vive-all the remnant in various capacities.

- They assist in overcoming helplessness and despair.
- They assist in ending a season of hope deferred.
- They aid in helping to end lengthy battles.
- They help bring God's supernatural strength to His people.
- They assist in firing up, encouraging, invigorating, and breathing resurrection life.
- They revive-them-all to stand on their feet, staking their place in the King's victorious army.
- They assist in reviving the remnant to take their place in the glorious church, for which the King is returning.

Holy Spirit is answering our prayers by deploying millions of angels to revive us, to reinvigorate the bride and fill their lamps with oil. The outpouring is a replenishing one, so the bride can take all she needs—there will be plenty more. The fresh winds of revival are blowing. I believe these revival angels are assisting Holy Spirit in the times of refreshing referred to in Acts 3:20.

Many of us have been through what seem to be times of desert heat, bleaching us to the bone. We've endured hot times when we've felt very dry, when it seemed our hope was gone and there was nothing left. We've seen our visions strewn about and disconnected in the desert valleys. We've been picked clean by opportunistic demon vultures, while satanic wolves have scattered our bones every which way. But Breath Spirit says the bones can live. Breath Spirit says, "Watch this. I'm bringing the breath of life to you and you'll come to life."

Re-vive-all angels are assisting Holy Spirit in breathing fresh life into God's people. They are aiding Holy Spirit strategy in strengthening and encouraging the remnant. No matter what the circumstance, no matter your condition, you can be revived.

REVIVAL SONGS

Old revival songs carry Holy Spirit wind upon them, teaching us new strategies of the Holy Spirit and helping us find treasured truth that assists us in interpreting the sacred Scriptures. There's a verity in the songs of old that can help train and disciple us for Kingdom of God purposes that will add the heart and passion of earlier movements and eras to this one, synergizing them together.

Jesus makes a statement in Matthew 13 in one of His parables that we need to pick up on. It adds inspiration, helping us to synergize past truths, revelations, anointings, and the passion and fire of those early revivals into our times, blending them into new Holy Spirit activity and what He is doing today. It's actually a Kingdom principle that adds things together so we can go to another level. It's designed to raise the bar. Jesus said in Matthew 13:52:

> *Therefore every teacher and interpreter of the Sacred Writings who has been instructed about and trained for the kingdom of heaven and has become a disciple is like a householder who brings forth out of his storehouse treasure that is new and [treasure that is] old [the fresh as well as the familiar]* (Matthew 13:52 AMPC).

There's still an anointing on those old revival songs of our mothers and fathers of faith. During the Second Great Awakening in the 1800s that was led by Charles Finney, Dwight L. Moody, Billy Sunday, and many others, there were several songs featured in the revivals that had been written by Fanny J. Crosby. Despite being totally blind, Fanny wrote over 8,000 songs during her lifetime. She had become blind by the time she was six months old, yet her songs painted vivid scenes, as though she was actually there. The name for that is hypotyposis—an ability to write as though you actually saw it yourself. Fanny wrote about the cross, the Lamb of God, mercy, and hope. She penned songs about golden streets as though she had actually been there. Songs and sermons about the cross were dominant in the Second Great Awakening. The idea of the times was simply this: the disciples who had gathered around the cross of Jesus had all run away, so we must learn to stay close to or near the cross, which the disciples eventually learned to do after Pentecost.

Due to Fanny's blindness, she had to memorize her 8,000 songs. She also memorized much of the Scripture and stories of the Bible. She wrote so many songs that she became famous locally around New York City and was invited to share her songs in the churches there.

One day, Fanny was invited to go to a prison in Manhattan to sing several of her songs and to share from the Scriptures she had memorized. One of the stories that she told is found in Matthew 20:29-34, about two blind beggars who were sitting by the road outside of Jericho. They heard that Jesus was passing by and started calling and shouting out, "Have mercy on us! Have mercy, Lord. Jesus, have mercy on us."

The crowds around Jesus told the beggars, "Be quiet! Jesus has people to call on; He has people to see. Be quiet." But the two beggars just pleaded even louder, "Jesus, have mercy on us. Don't pass us by." Of course, Jesus didn't pass them by. He stopped and healed their blindness.

Fanny Crosby, being herself blind, told that story with such passion and anointing and so vividly that men up and down the jail cells began to call out, "Jesus, don't pass us by. Do not pass me by." One man in particular, in a pleading, sobbing, wailing voice, shouted out very loudly, "Please, Jesus, do not pass me by."

On her way home that night from the Manhattan prison, Fanny said she couldn't get the man's desperate pleading out of her mind, so she wrote a song about it that very night, with his wailings echoing in her ears. It would be the song that actually made her famous, giving her worldwide acclaim, as Billy Sunday, Ira Sankey, Dwight L. Moody, and Charles Finney helped to make it heard. It was sung almost every night in the London revivals of the Second Great Awakening, and many times, people attending the revivals would shout out, "Jesus, please! Don't pass me by!"

I've been fortunate to have heard those old revival songs sung over a hundred or more times. My father was an evangelist, and until I was seven years old we were in one- and two-week revivals all the time. I heard those songs down in the Appalachian hills, amongst very poor people. Often, there wasn't even a piano—maybe just a guitar—but mostly they would just use their voices and sing with such feeling. The writers of those old revival songs meant for them to be felt. The anointing and the presence of God would be so real that sometimes, as a young boy, I'd be afraid to even move.

The Appalachian people stewarded those old revival songs, along with the black churches of America. The black churches kept the revival spirit in many of their songs. Their choirs of today reflect that spirit, and we need the wind on it, blowing revival through the land again. True revival is not a white revival. It's black, red, yellow, brown, and white—of every kindred, tribe, and tongue. We need the synergy of all the races, and we need the synergy of all the revival anointings. We need to plead for revival the way we used to. We need a gusher.

Following are the lyrics to the song Fanny Crosby wrote after visiting the Manhattan prison:

Pass Me Not, O Gentle Savior

by Frances J. Crosby, 1868

Pass me not, O gentle Savior,
Hear my humble cry;
While on others Thou art calling,
Do not pass me by.

Refrain:

Savior, Savior,
Hear my humble cry,
While on others Thou art calling,
Do not pass me by.
Let me at Thy throne of mercy
Find a sweet relief;
Kneeling there in deep contrition,
Help my unbelief.
Trusting only in Thy merit,
Would I seek Thy face;
Heal my wounded, broken spirit,
Save me by Thy grace.
Thou the spring of all my comfort,
More than life to me,
Whom have I on earth beside Thee,
Whom in Heav'n but Thee.

We need to get back to that kind of vividness again. There are so many who are in prisons, perhaps not a natural prison but those of other makings, and they're calling out, "Jesus, don't pass me by."

All over the earth, a division of re-vive-all angels is now activated to assist Holy Spirit in this new Pentecost era in reviving the remnant warriors. The infusion of fresh breath and fresh oil from Heaven has begun. Re-vive-all angels are moving under Holy Spirit leadership for the greatest revival in history.

Allow me to share this prophetic word from Lana Vawser, prophet and author based in Australia. This prophetic article speaks to angels of revival.

> While I was in the USA the Lord spoke to me about the visitation of a *revival angel* that is being released across the earth that is marking the season we are in. We are in a season of revival and it is beginning to build and sweep across the earth. The Lord was certainly highlighting the magnitude of the revival that will be seen on a global scale, yet I felt a real emphasis from the Lord on the body of Christ and individuals.
>
> As I sat with the Lord pondering what He spoke about this angel of revival, I was surrounded by the need for reviving, refreshment and rejuvenation within the body of Christ. As I sat with the Lord He spoke to me about encounters with the angels of revival that are going to increase more and more in this season, where the Lord is going to send these angelic hosts to minister to the people of God.

"Are not all angels ministering spirits sent to serve those who will inherit salvation?" (Heb. 1:14 NIV). We do not worship angels, we worship Jesus, but we must recognize that angels are ministering spirits that are sent to us. There were many, many other angels who were accompanying this angel of revival and they all had clocks in their hands. When I looked at the clocks all of them were at the same time—"midnight." As they came into the lives of believers they all sang in one accord "It's time! It's time! It's time! It's time for the *great revive!* It's time! It's time! It's time for the *great revive!*" These ministering angels were moving through the body of Christ, and I could hear Jesus giving them commands. They were commands that were scriptures on refreshment, breakthrough, on restoration, and the angels were moving according to the command of the Word of God. They were looking for the declaration from the people of God that was in line with the Word, His Word. As God's people declared the Word of God over their lives and circumstances, there was a great increase of the angelic activity in their lives.[2]

DECREES

1. WE DECREE new breath is entering God's people and a great army is rising.

2. WE DECREE dry bones, live!

3. WE DECREE we are being moved by Holy Spirit wind from the doldrums to new ports of blessing.

4. WE DECREE a billion-soul revival is coming.

5. WE DECREE hopelessness is bound, in Jesus' Name.

6. WE DECREE God's supernatural strength is being breathed into His people.

7. WE DECREE the fresh winds of revival are blowing.

8. WE DECREE we are a glorious church, not a glory-less church.

9. WE DECREE re-vive-all angels are assisting Holy Spirit in breathing fresh life into God's people.

10. WE DECREE break up, break out, break through, passover, and possess.

Notes

1. Robin Mark, "Revival," Revival in Belfast, CD (Hosanna!music, 1999).

2. For the complete word go to https://lanavawser.com/2016/04/07/here-it-is-the-angel-of-revival.

Chapter 9

ANGELS OF ALIGNMENT

The Lord gave me this message: "I knew you before I formed you in your mother's womb. Before you were born I set you apart and appointed you as my prophet to the nations."

"O Sovereign Lord," I said, "I can't speak for you! I'm too young!"

The Lord replied, "Don't say, 'I'm too young,' for you must go wherever I send you and say whatever I tell you. And don't be afraid of the people, for I will be with you and will protect you. I, the Lord, have spoken!" Then the Lord reached out and touched my mouth and said, "Look, I have put my words in your mouth! Today I appoint you to stand up against nations and kingdoms. Some you must uproot and tear down, destroy and over-throw. Others you must build up and plant."

Then the Lord said to me, "Look, Jeremiah! What do you see?"

And I replied, "I see a branch from an almond tree."

And the Lord said, "That's right, and it means that I am watching, and I will certainly carry out all my plans" (Jeremiah 1:4-12 NLT).

When Jeremiah was a young boy, God told him that prophetic words can uproot, tear down, destroy, and overthrow nations and kingdoms, but they can also build up and plant them. God also said, "Jeremiah, My prophetic words will carry out My plans. I have watched over My words to perform them." Other Bible translations state verse 12 this way:

- *"I am alert and active, watching over my word* to perform it" (AMPC).
- *"Thou hast well seen: for I will hasten my word to perform it"* (KJV).
- *"I'll make every word I give you come true"* (MSG).

I want to describe for you a particularly supernatural weekend that I experienced recently in Ann Arbor, Flint, and Detroit, Michigan. I've witnessed great miracles and healings—blind eyes opened, cripples walking, and diseases healed. Those are awesome in their own special way, but this was much different than anything I've ever seen in my life.

Back in 1994, Apostle Barbara Yoder and Prophet Chuck Pierce were doing a conference in Flint, Michigan where Prophet Chuck prophesied that the match for the greatest movement of God ever seen would be struck. He prophesied that when the match was struck, a revival fire would begin, traveling around this nation and continuing around the world. A Kingdom burning with glory would expand and then gain momentum, going from glory to glory.

Now, nearly 20 years later, God was again saying to go to Flint, strike the match, and do it before the end of the year, so we were scrambling to do this. The conference would be called "Strike the Match," and I was going to be there along with Apostle Barbara Yoder, Prophet Chuck Pierce, and my younger (only by 15 months) brother, Apostle Dutch Sheets. Neither Dutch nor I had ever heard the word Chuck had prophesied in 1994, but we trusted him and Barbara when they said that it was time to strike the match.

We started the weekend by first ministering at Apostle Barbara's church, Shekinah Church, in Ann Arbor, about 50 minutes from Flint. I spoke four times at Shekinah on how prophetic words intersect their moment, and how Holy Spirit uses angels to assist the words to come to pass. This has been a recurring theme of the Holy Spirit for several years now in my life, and I had been releasing this word throughout the nation. I knew it was to be declared everywhere I could, to prepare us for a new era. Thousands of prophetic words are connecting to their moment. It's not off in the future anymore. Heaven and the Kingdom of God are amped up and it's time that we get amped up, as well. I referred to the Strike the Match event as I taught, even though I didn't yet have a clear picture on the details of what we were going to do in Flint.

After ministering at Shekinah Church, we drove to Flint for the Strike the Match conference where I would finally get to hear Prophet Chuck's prophecy from 1994. Upon arriving at the conference, I began to sense Holy Spirit saying this would be a very strategic evening. I went on high alert in my spirit, as I felt that something of great significance was going to occur. You know when you have that feeling deep inside that something big is up—I had that sense.

Allow me to set this up from these verses in Isaiah in order to set a biblical foundation before we get to the details.

> *"I don't think the way you think. The way you work isn't the way I work." God's Decree. "For as the sky soars high above earth, so the way I work surpasses the way you work, and the way I think is beyond the way you think. Just as rain and snow descend from the skies and don't go back until they've watered the earth, doing their work of making things grow and blossom, producing seed for farmers and food for the hungry, so will the words that come out of my mouth not come back empty-handed. They'll do the work I sent them to do, they'll complete the assignment I gave them"* (Isaiah 55:8-11).

Notice that God's prophetic words, dreams, and visions to us have assignments that He has breathed upon them and they are empowered to do what He says when His people stand in faith for them. Prophetic words are connecting to their moment, corporately and individually. It is true for your life, your family, your business, vocation, and ministry; it is across the board. God's promises will connect to their moment.

In Daniel 9, we see this principle of prophetic words intersecting with their moment as prophetic prayers, strategies, and instructions concerning a new era play out in an extremely dramatic way. It's a prayer of Daniel that is instructive as well as fascinating. This is a prayer that absolutely changed history by changing a nation. It activated prophetic promises and caused Heaven to respond, and it caused the release of angel princes and their armies from Heaven. It is a prayer that bound a demon prince and overthrew his reign over an entire region. This is also exactly what we experienced in Flint.

We must understand that the Bible is not only a history of what has happened but is also instructive for today. We are in Holy Spirit times, just like Daniel or any of the prophets or apostles. They were not a different class of people than we are. They were in a spiritual realm that is available to us, as well. They were God's people, just as we are. Respect them, absolutely, but do not deify them. As born-again ones, we, too, are in Holy Spirit times of God-appointed, powerful angelic assistance. We can, and we should, experience supernatural Kingdom of God activity. Actually, because of a new covenant and the baptism of the Holy Spirit, we should experience it even more so.

Remember, Daniel was praying for wisdom concerning his nation and the future. God heard his prayer the first day he started praying and sent the angel, Gabriel, with the answer to that prayer. Gabriel said, "I'm here to help you understand the strategy that the King has for your future. There is a future and it is good. I'm here to assist and answer your prayers." Clearly, God assigns angels to answer prayers. They organize around the prayers of God's people, helping to bring them to pass—especially the prayers of an Ekklesia for a region or nation. Angels engage in spiritual warfare against hell's principalities and powers. They help us battle to bind princes that are trying to stop prayer, prophetic words, or the strategies of God for a new era.

Back to Flint: we were there to strike the match, as God had said. The service began and immediately started to get deep. The worship was so powerful and bold. I was seated on the front row between Prophet Chuck and Apostle Dutch, with the pulpit being only 15 or so feet away. The place was packed, holding around 500 on the main level, and it also had a balcony.

I began praying in the spirit and asking Holy Spirit, "Why am I here? I understood the assignment to teach in Ann Arbor, but why am I here? What am I to do? Am I to pray something? I'm available and I'm listening."

As I was praying this, the worship leader switched to a song about the Great I Am and the Great Awakening. The last line of the song was, "Why not here? Why not us? Why not now?" About the second time through the song, I looked up and saw the largest angel I have ever seen—just enormous. He was a huge angel prince of Holy Spirit and glowed with such power and God's glory.

The angel was dressed in gold and white apparel with a purple, or wine-colored, sash that wrapped around his neck, over his shoulder, and hung down below his waist. From studying angels and prophetic colors for the past decade, I knew what these colors meant. They are the colors in Scripture of government, power, authority, or dominion. This was a mighty angel prince, a being of great power of the Kingdom of Almighty God, that was now in our midst. I recall seeing his face glow with radiant confidence and commanding authority. His eyes were piercing and boldness was all over his countenance.

As I watched, this mighty angel dropped a very large plumb line over top of us. It was like a carpenter's plumb line, only much bigger, perhaps 20 feet long. Imagine a typical plumb line, magnified about 20 times. When the angel dropped the plumb line, I felt the whole place shift as if it had jolted into alignment. I knew that it was shifted in the spirit realm, but somehow I felt it in the natural. This is a concept I don't fully understand, but I felt it even though I knew it was in the spirit. I looked over at Prophet Chuck and said, "That huge angel just dropped a plumb line over us." He looked around and started shaking his head, saying, "I felt it come in. I felt it come in. The host is here. The host of Heaven has come in."

Worship continued and I wasn't sure what we were to do with this, but I knew something was about to happen. The whole place was electric at this point. Prophet Chuck got up to speak and began to share about the 1994 prophetic word. He described how his teaching that night had been about deliverance from demon curses, with one curse being the curse of death or a spirit of death. He talked about how, when he reached that point in his teaching, the spirit of death had attacked him by grabbing his throat, and he literally couldn't speak. The demon prince entrenched in Flint, Michigan tried to kill Prophet Chuck in front of everyone. All he could do was wave to Barbara, who was sitting up front, to come pray for him. She jumped up and ran to him, taking authority over the attack in Jesus' Name until he was free. Hundreds of people had seen this happen, and some of them were actually in attendance again on this night.

When Chuck was freed from the attack, he could then prophesy the word of the Lord with liberty in the region, and that word he prophesied in 1994 was, "A match would be struck in Flint and it would start a movement in the world that would not stop. A revival would begin to burn. A movement begins."

After Chuck shared what had happened in 1994, he called me up to share about the huge angel I had seen just a few moments before. As I described how the angel had dropped the plumb line over us, shifting things in the spirit realm, there was a shout that rose up from the leader who had organized and secured the location that we were using that night. Others who attended this church also began to shout. I had no idea what was going on, but they were certainly excited.

We discovered he was one of the pastors who had been on staff at that church for years, but had left in 2013 to travel America and other parts of the world, including China, because Holy Spirit told him to go and drop a plumb line in major cities declaring, "Come into alignment with King Jesus." He had been doing so for the past five years and had just returned from that assignment. He stood up and held up a plumb line that he carried in his pocket.

Of course, I had no idea and had never met this man, but a prophetic decree—a prophetic word, a prophetic act—was intersecting its moment and Holy Spirit and His angels were activating it. I knew in my spirit this word had just connected to its moment. You can't make this up; it was simply amazing.

After telling about the angel, I sat down and Prophet Chuck continued to speak. All of a sudden, this spirit of death attacked him again, like it did back in 1994. This demon prince, rooted in Flint, attacked him right in front of all of us and we watched it happen. Prophet Chuck grabbed his chest and throat area and he couldn't speak. He began to wave his hands again, like he had in 1994, for Apostle Barbara to come up. The only words I heard him say were, "It's happening." Dutch and I looked at each other and we were like, "Whoa!"

I want to emphasize that there was absolutely no fear in the room. It was like an atmosphere of faith and boldness had entered in. A bold confidence came into the room, like the fierce confidence that I had seen on the angel prince's face just a few moments earlier. We even talked later about the lack of fear. Our thinking was, "Oh, we're going to take care of this. You are done for in this region. You are going to be bound tonight. This demon attack will not stand and it's going to stop."

Apostle Barbara ran up to Chuck and began praying in the spirit and then binding that demon spirit in Jesus' Name as we all joined in. As we were praying, I heard the Holy Spirit say to me very clearly (it might have been out loud, I don't know; it was loud to me), "The windpipes of the prophetic must open and sound forth like a trumpet."

I ran up the steps, touched Prophet Chuck's throat, and prophesied the word of the Lord: "The windpipes of the prophetic are now being opened to sound forth like a trumpet.

The prophetic will now sound forth in the land at new levels like a trumpet. Open, open, open."

Then Apostle Barbara began to prophesy: "Hell will not shut the prophetic up and it's all going to go to a new level." While she was prophesying, I reached over and took the plumb line the former pastor was holding out to me and I held it over Prophet Chuck's head. He had his head back, as if he was looking up, but his eyes were closed.

At the end of the prophecy, he opened his eyes and saw the plumb line. He couldn't have missed it because it was right between his eyes. He shook his head back and forth and started prophesying into the new era, and then he started commanding the match to strike, commanding a new movement to move and burn. Apostle Dutch then came up and began declaring that the word of the Lord has come to a fullness of time, and he just kept talking about it—we're in the fullness of time. It was incredible; it was Bible; it was supernatural. We then took a huge match (about a yard long) that someone had made for the conference and we struck it, declaring, "A movement begins. Let revival fires burn. A revival fire will go forth until it goes around the world."

As we were doing this, the power across the river from where we were meeting went out. This was an area, known to Apostle Barbara and those that live there, that is notorious for its witchcraft. It actually has altars built to demons and satanists worship there. As we struck the match, the power in that part of town went out, while the rest of the town was fine. It made the news that night and they even said, "At this point, we do not know the reason for the power failure."

Afterward we all just looked at each other like, "Did that just happen?" I kept telling myself that this had actually happened; I was there. I told Carol at least 10 times that no one was going to believe me. It was absolutely amazing.

We were scheduled to meet the following morning with about 250 leaders back in Ann Arbor, with Chuck, Dutch, and me tag-teaming it. Following the service that night in Flint, I drove back to my hotel in Ann Arbor. I got to my room about 9:50 p.m., and I was so tired from speaking four times in Ann Arbor, then driving to Flint and taking part in a three-hour service, and then driving back to Ann Arbor. Not only that, but I had had the flu for four days and had, in fact, been to see the doctor the day before I left for Michigan.

When I arrived back at the hotel that evening, I thought, "I'm not going to turn the TV on and I'm not going out to eat with everybody. I'm going straight to bed," and I did. I was probably asleep by 10 p.m.—I was zonked. I didn't know that the supernatural night wasn't yet over, and something happened that night that has never happened to me before. Just after midnight, one of the angels that had been assigned to me when I accepted my calling to be an apostle, years ago in Indianapolis, physically shook me awake. He shook my left shoulder until he woke me up. I'm not talking figuratively. He literally put his hand on my shoulder and shook me. I barely woke up and then went right back to sleep. Again, I felt a hand on my left shoulder, shaking me. I woke up, but went back to sleep again. For the third time, I felt the hand on my shoulder, shaking me. Finally, I truly awakened, thinking, "I'm the only person in this room."

I sat up and looked at the clock; it was 12:10 a.m. Then, amazingly, I saw the angel of the Lord. He said to me, "The Lord says the plumb line prophecy has intersected its moment." I began thinking, "Plumb line prophecy? What's the plumb line prophecy?" Then I remembered. At the end of 2016 and the beginning of 2017, I had recurring visions of angels dropping plumb lines over hundreds of apostolic hubs around the world. The angels holding the plumb lines were meticulously aligning each hub with their assignment for the region. Each hub represented something different regarding the vision the Lord had given them. Their assignments and how they were to be accomplished were different from one another, and the alignment had to be exactly right.

I had seen this same vision at least a dozen times and I had also given a prophetic word from the vision concerning the new era and the third great awakening. Now, a few years later, the angel of the Lord had shaken me awake, stating that the plumb line prophecy had intersected its moment. I was wide awake by that time, so I got up and opened my briefcase, emptying it out and going through every note. It was the middle of the night and I had stuff all over the bed as I searched through everything to see if I had the prophecy with me. I finally found it and started to read through it, and as I did I saw that things Dutch had said earlier that evening were in the prophecy. He had talked about hovering glory and he just kept going on and on about it. I remembered thinking, as he was saying it, "Why are you saying it over and over?"

As I continued reading this prophetic word, I saw it included things that Apostle Barbara had just prophesied and that Prophet Chuck had just said a few short hours ago. I knew I was supposed to read it the next morning at the leaders' meeting, which I did. I met with Barbara, Chuck, and Dutch right before the meeting and was going to tell them what had happened the night before, and when I came in the room, Barbara said, "You're not going to believe this. I got home last night and just a little bit after 12 o'clock, I turned on the news and they were talking about the power outage in Flint."

I said, "Well, you're not going to believe this. A little after 12 o'clock last night, the angel of the Lord shook me awake and reminded me of a prophetic word." The angel of the Lord said it had intersected its moment and that everything would now accelerate in Christ's Kingdom.

Here is that word:

> The spirit says to the church, I am aligning Heaven with earth to open the birth canal of My Kingdom. It is open, says the Lord. The breaches have been turned. Welcome to calving season. Welcome to the season of awesome birthings. Welcome to the season of greater and greater and even greater glory. A new degree of glory is now rising over My remnant, and from hovering glory My Spirit is moving to birth plans, purposes, transitions, and ministries that have been incubating in My presence. Welcome to hatching season. Welcome to the season of ever-increasing glory. My glory will now be revealed from one degree of glory to another degree of glory to yet another degree of glory. From glory to glory to glory

to glory to glory to glory. Pulsating glory will now throb from the throne of the King of Glory. Out rays of glory have been amped up, as now more and more of who I really am will be revealed. Yes, Savior; yes, Healer; yes, Deliverer; but, yes, King of Kings; yes, Lord of Lords; yes, Governing King. Wave after wave after wave of every increasing glory has now begun. Surge after surge after surge of My power and presence will now be seen. Welcome to the surge of the King of Glory.

Omnipotent, strident forces have now been released and hell cannot prevail. The forever loser will bow. Welcome to the victory surge of the King of Glory. Welcome to converged ages. Welcome to the blended anointings into greater multifaceted anointings. Welcome to the combined anointings of history. Welcome to the King's anointing upon heirs at destined levels. For you are entering the season of My tangibly real, manifest glory. My presence will be seen, pulsating on an un-compromised remnant at levels never seen before.

For as I have shown through the ages, My hovering glory is the womb of gestation for what My Spirit moves to birth on the earth. For just as the earth was born from hovering glory as My spirit brooded, moved, and incubated to bring to birth the sun, the moon, the stars, the earth, the animals, man himself, and mandated dominion government; and just as transition and transformation and deliverance and new increased Kingdom government and laws, new leaders, and a whole new generation of heirs was birthed from hovering glory in the Exodus. Just as promises made were accelerated to fullness— here is your Promised Land. Here's what I promised. I watched over My word and I have performed it. Just as from hovering glory shining around Mary and Joseph, a King and a Kingdom was born. From glory's womb, My Spirit birthed a new Kingdom's government on the earth. From glory that shone round about them, the ministry of angels increased at higher and higher levels than ever before. Angel choirs sang. Angel messengers activated. Angel princes protected.

And just as from hovering glory, Holy Spirit sat brooding, moving, incubating over the remnant in Acts chapter 2, birthing the New Testament church, birthing new gifts; birthing new heirs; birthing a new apostolic and prophetic generation; birthing new leaders young, old, male, female; birthing new levels of ministry; birthing fivefold ministry at levels never ever seen before; birthing yet another level of angelic ministry; birthing a new level of Kingdom power, authority, and government in My Name; so you are now moving into another season of greater glory.

My glory has been hovering, and My womb is full. My Spirit has been brooding, incubating for decades, to complete gestation of promises now due. It is your due season. For you are entering the birthing season of My great awakening, and now will be birthed what previous hoverings have birthed, only at higher and higher and higher and then higher levels. Supernatural deliverance is being birthed at greater degrees than ever before. Promises are being birthed at greater levels than ever before. Transformative reformation will now be birthed. Miracles and healings are being birthed at far greater levels. New leaders will now be birthed. Joshuas and Calebs will rise to prominence. Stephens, Phillips, Ruths, and Esthers will rise to prominence. A whole new generation of believers will now be born again. A new Jesus movement far greater than the '70s will be born from the womb of greater glory.

The millennials will possess the land. New heirs are rising to their position of inheritance. A Joshua generation will rise to cross over and possess My promise. Radical millennials have been brooded upon in protective custody of Holy Spirit who has shielded them from unbelieving wilderness wanderers. Their angels are now connecting them with their destinies. Now ever-increasing glory will reflect from them like sunlight upon mirrors. They will not be the lost generation. Rather, they will be the Lord's valor army, war eagles flying in alignment. My Ekklesia will now function at higher and higher levels. It will rule and it will reign with Me as intended. A new level of ruling power is now being birthed. Dominating authority over hell's kingdom is now being birthed and activated at levels never seen before. Authority given to heirs will now function at destined levels as My glory surges.

Greater degrees of fivefold ministry are now being born, activated, functioning, and empowering. An apostolic-prophetic generation will now be seen. Equipping wisdom is being born. Strategies are being born in apostolic hubs everywhere. The gospel of My Kingdom will be preached and from the womb of greater and greater glory, My Spirit has brooded, moved, and incubated to bring to birth the greatest harvest in all of time. The gestation period has ended, says the Lord. It is birth season. It is your due season. Welcome to the surge of the King of Glory. For the angels are declaring from the heavens, no more delay, no more delay, no more delay.

Angels of alignment are working with us to connect apostolic hubs with their assignments. We will see this division of angel armies playing a critical role in keeping the true church on the cutting edge of what Holy Spirit is saying in this great new Pentecost era.

These angels of alignment are aligning the Ekklesia for revival fires to burn and go around the world. Here is an article from Julie Myer concerning angels of alignment and revival:

I looked up through the ceiling and saw a vast angelic army. Together the angels seemed like an ocean of brilliant, radiant light. It appeared they were pulsing and trembling, just waiting to break in. They were waiting to be released by the call of the angel who had led me into the room. He was in great anguish because he earnestly desired to give the call they were all expecting, but he only said one sentence: "It is not quite time yet."

I kept looking at the heavenly hosts. I could see ladders. I could see lamps. I could feel the anticipation and how strongly they wanted to break in. The angelic multitude was getting ready to burst in, not with a simple entrance, but with a flood of divine activity. Only this single angel held back the imminent breakthrough.

But it was not quite time for him to release them. There was something yet to be completed before the breakthrough could happen, though I was not shown what it was.

This was part of a dream I had back in 2007.

I have recently had another dream I believe is a continuation of this first dream, for I was given instructions in this dream and told to cry out for help from the sanctuary. I was told to cry out for the "angels of revival." And so I cry out and share this new dream with you, because God is listening.

I had a dream, I was told to call forth the "angels of revival." I was told to call for them three times. So I put my hand up to my mouth and began to shout: "I call forth the angels of revival. I call forth the angels of revival. I call forth the angels of revival." Suddenly, angels began to rise out of the mountains. Their bodies stood up out of the mountains. They were so huge.

These angels of revival were wearing golden robes that went down to their feet, and they had a cream colored collar around their neck. They were shining and they were singing. This beautiful choir, these beautiful harmonies...I could see the vibrations of their tones going forth and going out striking hearts. They were singing of the glories of God, and this tone, these songs, these vibrations of sounds, were going out of the building where I was and drawing in multitudes. This sound was drawing in the lost, the broken, and the sick.[1]

The match has been struck. It is time for worldwide revival. The angels of alignment are aligning the apostolic hubs for this awesome move of God.

DECREES

1. WE DECREE the match has been struck and revival fire will burn around the world.

2. WE DECREE angels of alignment are aligning apostolic hubs for their purposes.

3. WE DECREE angels are helping us understand the strategy of King Jesus for our future.

4. WE DECREE the windpipes of the prophetic will open and sound forth like a trumpet.

5. WE DECREE angels are organizing around the prayers of God's people, helping to bring them to pass.

6. WE DECREE great boldness to speak truth is coming upon the Ekklesia.

7. WE DECREE angels are dropping plumb lines to align the Ekklesia for the purposes Holy Spirit intends.

8. WE DECREE Holy Spirit is aligning Heaven with earth to open the birth canal of the Kingdom of God.

9. WE DECREE the forever loser will bow.

10. WE DECREE break up, break out, break through, passover, and possess.

NOTE

1. Julie Meyer, "Call Forth the Angels of Revival," The Elijah List, May 25, 2015, https://www.facebook .com/TheElijahList/photos/call-forth-the-angels-of -revivaljulie-meyermay-21-2015-oh-my-dove-in-the -clefts-/10153891954768989.

Chapter 10

ANGELS OF HEALINGS AND MIRACLES

The angel divisions of healings and miracles are activating for our times. At the beginning of 2013, I began to have a recurring vision. In the vision, I saw land oil pumps, like you see in the countryside, pumping oil. The lever on these pumps goes up and down, up and down, over and over. However, in my vision, it wasn't a lever doing the pumping—it was an angel. After seeing this vision several times, Holy Spirit spoke to me, saying, "These are angels of healings and miracles. They are pumping the old healing wells and opening new ones."

That really spoke to me because of my heritage. My father was a healing evangelist and I have been around healing evangelists all my life. I have seen so many miraculous healings. No one could ever tell me miracles aren't real; I've seen them with my own eyes. When my brother, Dutch, and I were about 12 and 13 years old, we were the "catchers" at the altar. Part of our assignment was to clean up the cancers that were left on the floor after people were healed. We used to go to church early on Wednesday nights because people would sometimes be brought to the service in ambulances to be prayed for. We would hold open the doors and help push them in on their stretchers. That probably wouldn't even be allowed to take place today, but back then it did.

Gordon Lindsay, founder of Christ for the Nations and my father's friend, used to come to our house when I was a young boy. Oral Roberts preached for my dad way back in the day, in a little Pentecostal church. I was just a kid, running around the parsonage while the evangelists would be preaching, and I would just be waiting for church to be over so I could go home and watch TV, and there would be Oral Roberts in our home after the service. Evangelists A.A. Allen, David Nunn, T.L. Osborne—I was raised around these men, just as some of your children are raised around today's ministers. I saw so many miracles, it was ingrained into me that God can do any-thing. I would believe that anyway, because it's God's Word, but it's at a different level for me because I truly saw miracles take place. At one point, when my dad was pastoring a little church of about 30 to 45 people, he and other local pastors would get together and have a summer revival. They would pray for the sick and, again, Dutch and I would be the "catch-ers" at the meetings.

One time we were at a small church in Hamilton, Ohio and there were around 40 people in attendance. We had to sit on the front row because Dutch was always goofing off and Dad didn't trust us to sit anywhere else. At this particular meeting, something happened I will never forget as long as I live. A man in a wheelchair was pushed up to the front row where we were sitting. He was completely twisted up, like a pretzel. Three of the local preachers gathered around him, praying in the spirit, and I could hear bones begin to pop, like when a chiropractor works on you. That man began to unwind in his chair and then jumped up onto his feet. He was totally healed, and I will never forget watching that take place.

The Holy Spirit is activating angels to uncap the old healing wells. Many years ago, in the early days of The Oasis Church, Benny Hinn came to use our facility to conduct a meeting. Carol and I were sitting on the platform with some other guest ministers as Benny began to minister. This, too, is something I will never, ever forget. A little girl, maybe 11 or 12 years old, came up to the platform and joined the line of people waiting for Benny to pray for them. She had one beautiful blue eye, while the other eye was completely white, with no pupil. I was sitting only three feet away from her. Benny said for everyone to reach their hands out toward her and pray, and as they did I watched as a black dot appeared in her eye, and then the most beautiful blue you have ever seen. She began to cry out, "I can see!" There was no faking this; I saw it.

Not long after that, we experienced an incredible miracle in our church family. A young man around 18 years old, who attended the church and was on our basketball team, had gone in for minor surgery on his back. During the surgery, something or somebody messed up, nicked his spine, and he was paralyzed from the waist down. Such devastation. His parents had to push him into the services in a wheelchair. We had prayed for him numerous times, anointed him with oil, and fasted—all with unseen results.

One Saturday morning, I was in my office preparing for Sunday service when I sensed a change in the atmosphere. I put my pen down and said, "Lord, what?" I knew something was happening. I started praying in the spirit and walked into the balcony of our church. I didn't know what else to do, but I knew to put my spiritual antennas up and listen. The angel of the Lord, one of the angels that accompanies my life, spoke to me and said, "Tomorrow morning, announce that the healing power of the Lord will fall in the room like rain."

That Sunday morning, the worship just exploded. I got up and announced what the angel of the Lord had said to me, and when I did, hundreds of people just fell back onto their pews. It was like a wave, and as I looked over the sanctuary I saw this young man in the wheelchair. I said to him, "Today is the day. Get up and walk." He started to shake, like someone with palsy would, and began trying to get up. He finally stood up and the whole house went crazy. He's standing and shaking, and then starts trying to walk. He looked like a mummy with stilted movement. After about his third step, he was completely loose and began to run all across the front of the church. He continued running and then jumped into the arms of one of our staff pastors, totally healed. We have pictures of him holding the wheelchair above his head. We also have a letter from his doctor, who didn't call it a miracle but stated that medically this was impossible. Same thing!

Again, angels are opening the old healing wells. After having the vision, we gathered as many intercessors as we could and went to every place in Ohio that we knew of that had held healing meetings over the years. We have walked the grounds of those meeting places and have asked God to open those wells. Spring up, oh wells!

> *For an angel of God went down at a certain time into the pool and stirred up the water; then whoever stepped in first, after the stirring of the water, was made well of whatever disease he had* (John 5:4 NKJV).

These angels are still stirring the waters. We have moved into this new era, a season when angels are uncapping old healing wells and opening new ones, and when miracles are going to accelerate. Let these testimonies build your faith.

NINA DANCHO: FROM THE KEYSTONE STATE OF PENNSYLVANIA

Apostle Tim, my appreciation for all that I've been receiving of comfort, encouragement, and perspective by tuning in to The Oasis broadcasts. At the end of the May 3, 2020 program, you prayed at the end for those who needed healing. I placed my niece's husband (Dean) picture up to the computer screen. He had been hospitalized for over a week at that time while being tested for COVID, among other things. The doctors had said without a miraculous intervention they were going to have to go in to determine what was not working. He was considered high risk because of prior blood clots. They finally determined it was a bowel blockage. Apostle Tim prayed for people and specifically that the Breaker would break us through. That night, the NG tube came out on its own! They gave Dean liquids and his blockage was dissolved. He is now healed and was released just two days later—glory to God! Breakthrough!

MEL SHAFFER

On October 27, 2017, I had a routine blood test with my family doctor that showed a low platelet count and anemia, and he recommended I see a hematologist to determine the cause. In January of 2018, after becoming lightheaded, I threw up a large amount of blood and went to the hospital ER. While waiting on test results I got up to go to the restroom and I felt like my legs were as heavy as lead and stuck to the floor. I felt as if I was leaving my physical body; I felt I was dying. I heard Holy Spirit tell me to decree the word of God over myself and I decreed Psalm 118:17, "I will not die but live and declare the works of the Lord." With a nurse's help I made it back to the bed and then my diagnosis was delivered—I had cirrhosis of the liver. I thought they had made a mistake, I had not consumed any alcohol for 35 years.

Many tests were done, working around the bleeding I was experiencing. One test showed I had bleeding varices caused from blood backing up in my body, not being able to flow through the liver scarring. Throughout January of 2018 I experienced many problems associated with my hospital treatment and the disease of cirrhosis. On February 2, the day of our Annual Prophetic Summit at The Oasis, I was upset because I had been told I was heading toward a liver transplant. I remember telling Pastor Carol I did not want a transplant and she reminded me I should not limit how God would choose to heal me. This was the first time I had any peace about the possibility of surgery.

One Sunday in February or March of 2018, Pastor Tim spoke about the difference between a *rhema* and *logos* word of God; I asked God to give me a *rhema* word for my situation. I expected a word about healing, but what I received was more perfect than I could have imagined:

"I will withhold no good thing from you" (see Ps. 84:11).

"Peace, be still" (see Ps. 46:10).

In March 2018, I had a needle biopsy of my liver as they were still trying to find the cause. Throughout March and April, I had endoscopy with banding, and I was told by the ER doctor that the liver had gotten significantly worse—much more than they would have expected during such a short period of time. At that time, I was given a choice of Cleveland Clinic, Ohio State University, or University of Cincinnati for a liver transplant. On May 1, I had blood work done again, and when the doctor got my results and saw how high my counts were she called me and told me to immediately go to UC's ER, and my appointment at the transplant center was moved up. On May 15—another endoscopy; every time I had this done until my healing I had to have at least three varices banded and sometimes more. The bandings go around the varices to keep them from filling with blood, which causes the bleeding.

On May 30, 2018, I was finally given the diagnosis that explained the reason I had developed cirrhosis—Congenital Hephatic Fibrosis, a rare (one in 10,000 to 20,000) genetic problem that causes abnormally small veins in the liver that constrict and leave scarring.

On June 3, I returned to Kettering Hospital after passing out at home. I had strep-bovid, which can be common in liver patients. This led to sepsis. During this time our fourth grandchild was born and I wondered if I would ever meet her. The infection had caused an irregular EKG; thankfully, my heart was not damaged. By this time, I had lost about 30 pounds; my husband, Dave, had become my full-time caretaker; I was very weak, requiring occupational and physical therapy at home; I was not allowed to go up/down stairs; and I could barely shower and get dressed, stopping to rest in between.

At this point I was also tested for cancer of the pancreas, which I did *not* have, thankfully! My numbers were high because of the infection so the test that was done had a false result.

June 24 I had to have a colonoscopy in preparation for transplant surgery; I had that done and went home just to wait for a liver. However, that night I spiked a fever, 104.3, and had to go back to the UC Hospital. I was admitted for nine days while they looked for the source of the infection, which was never found but the fever continued until I was finally dismissed. While hospitalized there were more scans, another MRI, more heart testing, and then they took out the PICC line thinking it could have been the source. During this time Pastor Tim and Carol came to pray with us, and Carol suggested Dave and I take communion together. Dave was able to find crackers and juice from the nurse and we took communion in the hospital room.

July 16, 2018: My "Suddenly" Healing

We had an appointment at the transplant center later that day. As I was taking a shower it occurred to me that I felt better than I had for a very long time. I soon realized color had returned to my face. Dave even teased me that if I went to the transplant center looking that good they might not give me a liver. We laughed but didn't realize the truth we were about to see. My blood test results were greatly improved. The transplant coordinator said she could not explain it because what I had "Would not just go away, there is no cure." I told her I knew God had healed me.

Right after this, our worship pastor, Rachel Shafer, gave a message about *suddenlies*. I wanted to jump up and confirm that what she had heard God say was true indeed and that I had just experienced my own suddenly. I decided to wait for official confirmation. I continued to improve, getting stronger literally day by day. I was able to work in my flower beds, wash windows, and no longer needed home therapy to get stronger. On July 30, I had my first endoscopy that did not require any banding of varices, and I have had three since then, all good with no banding.

The doctors wanted to keep me on the transplant list while they continued to monitor my condition with tests, but eventually they marked me "inactive," and finally they removed me from the list. Dave asked my doctor if he had ever seen anything like this happen before. His response was yes but he couldn't explain it. I told him I could—*God healed me!* This past January, 2019 was my last appointment at the transplant center; they released me as a patient and took me off the transplant list.

I had peace that I would be alright, no matter what, and even Pastor Carol said to me once—*but God*. I am amazed at what God has done for me. So many prayed for me, our church and friends, pastors. Ephesians 3:20-21 sums it up for me: "Now to Him who is able to do immeasurably more than all we ask or imagine according to His power that is at work within us—to Him be glory in the church and in Christ Jesus throughout all generations, forever and ever! Amen."[1]

RACHEL SHAFER (JAIDIN'S TESTIMONY)

A couple of years ago, our youngest son, Jaidin, had a very serious brain bleed. Jaidin was born with a cleft lip and palate and was having a surgery related to that. During the surgery, he had a stroke which affected much of his body. His muscles and head control were very weak. Prior to surgery, he was a healthy, active, spunky, fun-loving boy and after the stroke he couldn't walk or sit up on his own and he was being fed through a feeding tube. It was heart-breaking. He was sad, mad and frustrated. And we were, too.

We went through a very intense time of praying and contending for his healing. There were many things we were praying and believing for concerning healing he needed throughout his body. After almost a month of being in the hospital, we had begun to see some improvement with Jaidin's strength, but we were extremely concerned with his swallow.

He simply wasn't swallowing at all. He couldn't even swallow his own saliva. His brain bleed had occurred in the place that controlled the swallowing mechanism. He had a suction tube and he suctioned out his mouth constantly. When he was away from the suction machine, he carried a cup that he could spit into because he could not swallow it. The doctors eventually put a patch on his neck to dry up his secretions, so that he wouldn't have to use the suction machine quite as much.

It was really hard because Jaidin desperately wanted to eat and drink again. It was hard for him to understand why he couldn't do that anymore. While we were in the hospital, he made a list of all the things he wanted and was always having me add food items to his grocery shopping list. At the top of his list were Pringles and pepperoni pizza.

After quite some time in the hospital, we were eventually moved to the rehab floor. This is where patients go who are expected to be there for a while. Many patients on this floor had been there for some time, as rehab is a process, not a quick fix, and several of them had become good friends. Often, the patients on the rehab floor would get together and hang out in one of the larger rooms.

There was a party organized one night for that year's Super Bowl that included food. We had been very careful to not eat in Jaidin's room, as it just seemed so unfair to him. He really wanted to go to this party, though. I took him that night and it was just incredibly sad. He was wheeled into the room in his wheelchair because at the time he was still unable to walk, and there was a table of food set up. I couldn't help myself; I let Jaidin take a couple licks of an Oreo. You should have seen his face light up! It caused me to tear up watching him.

Day after day, I just continued to do what I knew to do, what I've been taught. I tried very hard to preface my updates by saying, "The doctors say" or "the report says," so that it wouldn't seem as if I was agreeing with it.

I was quoting all the "good" scriptures like:

There has never been the slightest doubt in my mind that the God who started this great work in you would keep at it and bring it to a flourishing finish (Philippians 1:6).

We had many people all over the nation praying for Jaidin. One night, a scripture was prayed over him from Isaiah. I wrote it down on yellow construction paper with a green crayon and posted it in Jaidin's hospital room: "You [Jaidin] shall eat the good of this land" (Isa. 1:19).

This became a daily, often multiple times a day, decree over Jaidin. We decreed these specific words from scripture over him. And I would say to him, "You can swallow," and he would repeat back, "I can swallow." Every time he suctioned his mouth because he couldn't swallow, I would decree it again.

One evening, Jaidin told me that Jesus sent all the white angels to circle around his hospital bed and pray. I believe when he said "white angels" that he was probably seeing angels as light beings. I have no doubt that Jaidin had encounters with God while in the hospital.

And then the time came: God was going to watch over His Word to perform it. Six days after we had been decreeing the scripture from Isaiah, Mark was at the hospital and I was home. I got a phone call from Jaidin, and he simply said, "Mom, I swallowed." I made him repeat himself. I made my husband, Mark, tell me again and then I made the swallow therapist get on the phone, too.

Jaidin had swallowed a very small amount of water, but it was all the proof we needed that healing was taking place. It was a spark of hope that we were so desperate for. Some miracles are instant, but some are grown in the atmosphere of faith over time.

Thankfully, Jaidin has been completely healed. And yes, the first thing we went shopping for were Pringles and pepperoni pizza! God proved Himself faithful. He is a miracle working God![2]

Not all healing is physical, there are also emotional healings and healings of the soul and the mind. My daughter, Rachel, and her husband, Mark, have adopted two children with special needs from China—Lily and Jaidin. They brought Lily home from China when she was 14 months old, shortly before Christmas.

Carol and I consider it our job to spoil the kids at Christmas, showering them with lots of presents. Of course, Lily had never opened Christmas presents before. Her older sister, Maddie, who was seven, had opened lots of them and was frantically opening them at our house on Christmas Eve. But Lily was just sitting and watching, not really knowing what to do. Maddie began picking things out around the house that we already owned to give us for Christmas. She wrapped them, using gobs of tape, and brought them to us to open.

Lily, seeing this, began to play with the tape, instead of opening presents. I was watching all of this intently. When she was done playing with the tape, she tried to set it down but of course the tape stuck to her hand. She then reached over with her other hand and grabbed the tape and tried to set it down with that hand but again the tape stuck to her hand. She did this several times, growing increasingly more frustrated to the point of tears, not being able to get rid of the tape. Seeing her frustration, I took the tape away and we taught her how to open presents. She became a pro instantly.

I woke up in the middle of the night with God speaking to me about accumulated grief. I had never thought about the concept of grief accumulating, but the more I thought about it the more I realized it does happen. The older you get, the more grief in life seems to accumulate. This happens, that happens, and you think you've laid it down but really it's still sticking to the soul and you need someone bigger than you to come along and take it away.

Thankfully, the promise of our great Lord Jesus is that He came to take away grief that accumulates—the divorce, the loss of a loved one, the bankruptcy, the broken relationship. These things can accumulate in our lives, but Jesus comes to unwrap our soul and set us free, healing our emotions, feelings, and minds.

THIS HAPPENS, THAT HAPPENS, AND YOU THINK YOU'VE LAID IT DOWN BUT REALLY IT'S STILL STICKING TO THE SOUL AND YOU NEED SOMEONE BIGGER THAN YOU TO COME ALONG AND TAKE IT AWAY.

Many today need to be healed in their souls. They're walking around with taped hearts that only Jesus can set free. Thankfully, these divisions of angels that assist with healings and miracles are opening the old healing wells. They are also opening new wells of healings and miracles. Angels are assisting Holy Spirit to activate the King's anointing to heal, established through the stripes on Jesus' back, at levels the world has never seen before. You will see miracles accelerate. You will see healing accelerate in the physical realm, and you will see dramatic healings of the soul.

DECREES

1. WE DECREE healings are accelerating, in Jesus' Name.
2. WE DECREE miracles are accelerating, in Jesus' Name.
3. WE DECREE angels are pumping the old healing wells and opening new ones.

4. WE DECREE that God's healing power will fall like rain everywhere.

5. WE DECREE, *"Spring up, oh wells."*

6. WE DECREE the world is a pool of Bethesda; angels of healing and miracles are stirring the waters.

7. WE DECREE the suddenlies of the Holy Spirit will manifest in New Testament churches.

8. WE DECREE our emotions, minds, and souls are free, in Jesus' Name.

9. WE DECREE accumulated grief is being removed from the body of Christ.

10. WE DECREE break up, break out, break through, passover, and possess.

Notes

1. Medically documented miracle.

2. This excerpt is taken from Rachel Shafer's book *Expect God*. For further reading and information go to www .rachelshafer.com.

Chapter 11

ANGELS OF EVANGELISM

Another division of angels that can assist the believer was revealed to me several years ago—angels of evangelism. I was awakened in the middle of the night by someone shouting out, "Naphtali!" Carol was asleep, so I wasn't sure who could be doing the yelling. I drifted back to sleep and, once again, I heard "Naphtali!" It still wasn't clicking, but then I heard it a third time, and it sounded as if it was in surround sound. It didn't seem to be coming from downstairs or another room. It was a word that surrounded me: "Naphtali!" and I bolted upright in bed. It sounded as though it could be a Hebrew word, but I didn't recognize it at the time, because I was thinking it was a word for something—perhaps an object—and not someone's name.

I recognized the voice as one of the angels that had been assigned to me when I received my apostolic calling, and I was suddenly wide awake. I went downstairs and flipped through my concordance because I had recalled that Naphtali was one of the twelve tribes of Israel, which meant he was one of the sons of Jacob (who was later renamed Israel). I read in Genesis

49:20 that Jacob was bestowing a blessing to each of his sons, with Naphtali receiving his blessing in verse 21. I said, "Holy Spirit, talk to me, give me understanding." He then said, "Your apostolic hub, that I want you to build, will parallel the tribe of Naphtali."

I had never heard anything like this in my life. I've heard some teach that an apostolic hub will sometimes parallel one of the seven churches that are described in Revelation. I can understand that. However, I had never heard anyone suggest that a hub might parallel one of the twelve tribes. But God was very clear: "Your apostolate will parallel the tribe of Naphtali, taking on its flavor and characteristics."

Please understand that this experience was somewhat unusual for me. I'm a very structured person, and I like to think things through. I like line upon line, precept upon precept. I want to know who, what, when, where, why, how, and what car they drove to get there. That's just me. But having said that, I know that God has an audible voice, as do the angels. Unfortunately, many in our church world today don't think that way and, as a result, Holy Spirit strategies are hindered. If Jesus, the apostle Paul, the early church, and the patriarchs needed angels to assist them, then we certainly need them as well.

Here are several verses referencing those who heard the audible voice of God or of an angel:

- 1 Samuel 3:4—Samuel
- 1 Kings 19—Elijah
- Matthew 17:5—Jesus

  - Acts 9:4—Apostle Paul

Angels also spoke to Mary, Zachariah, Abraham, Daniel, Gideon, Joshua, Moses, and many others.

I then got out my lexicons and looked up the first time that *Naphtali* is used in Scripture (law of first use). I found it in Genesis 30:8: "Then Rachel said, 'With great wrestlings I have wrestled with my sister, and indeed I have prevailed.' So she called his name Naphtali" (NKJV).

Naphtali was a son of Jacob through Rachel's maid, Bilhah. The name *Naphtali* means "my wrestling" or "to twine, twist, or tie up." It also means to struggle, or a torturous, gut-wrenching type wrestling. Wrestling concerning barrenness and a new generation of children was what this was about.

For the past two decades or so, there has been a wrestling to birth the new movement of the apostolic and the prophetic. There has been a great season of barrenness. It has been a torturous wrestling and gut-wrenching at times. Because it was not accepted well, the warfare against it was very difficult. However, Holy Spirit has brought us to a place of a new birthing and a new move of God. You can feel it rising all over the world. This movement is about birthing new sons and daughters in the Kingdom of God.

I was aware that God was trying to tell me something, so I just kept asking, "Lord, what?" I sat there for perhaps an hour or so, meditating on what He had said, but I had no idea what it all meant. I pondered this for several weeks and bounced it off those I thought could offer some perspective. They all agreed it was significant, but they didn't have any real insight. Because an angel of the Lord had spoken in an audible voice to me, I just couldn't let it go, and finally prophetic revelation and guidance began to come. A pattern of enlightenment began to emerge that grew into a strategy that we could begin to implement. I knew this was a word for us and the amazing prophetic parallel concerning the tribe of Naphtali and the church was becoming clear.

NINE PROPHETIC PARALLELS

In my research, I found nine distinctive parallels that prophecy to the body of Christ. I would have never thought of this in a million years had not the angel emphasized "Naphtali" to me. I don't typically think this way, but I began to think that apostolates could possibly be mantled like one of the 12 tribes. This was new understanding for me at the time.

1. Genesis 49:21

Before Jacob died, he called his 12 sons in and blessed them. He declared, "Naphtali is a deer let loose. He giveth goodly words producing magnificent fawns." The Hebrew commentaries tell us that this is referencing the poetic and the speaking characteristics of the tribe of Naphtali. They were great communicators.

The meaning of the phrase is dual in the Hebrew language. It means "producing lovely fawns," which would represent new births. It also carries the concept of producing lovely words, meaning communication is good and clear to produce magnificent fawns.

A fawn, which is a young deer in its first year, represents the coming generation. I began to hear the Lord say it was time to produce magnificent fawns, or communicators, for the Kingdom of God. Like the tribe of Naphtali, we are to produce a coming generation of excellent communicators. Since receiving that word, I have begun to steer things that way, synergizing and working with the coming generations of young men and women.

I called a special meeting one evening of those who could further strategize with me concerning what this word, *Naphtali*, was all about. We met upstairs in our church's conference room and spent several hours praying, strategizing, and talking about the meaning and application of this word.

As we prepared to leave at the end of the evening, we looked out of the conference room window, and right beneath it were two fawns with white spots on their back. For as many years as we have been in that location, I had never seen anything like that. What are the chances that on the night we came together and strategized about what to do concerning the magnificent fawns, that two actual fawns would show up under that window? Obviously, it was a confirmation from the Lord that we were to raise the coming generation to be excellent communicators.

2. *Ezekiel 48:34*

This tells us Naphtali was a gate to the city of Jerusalem on the west side. The earthly city of Jerusalem had 12 gates, with each gate named after one of the tribes of Israel, the sons of Jacob. I began to hear Holy Spirit say that the Ekklesias are to be gates of the Kingdom of God in their regions. We are to be a gate of Heaven, a place where angels ascend and descend. Naphtali's father, Jacob, in Genesis 28 is the one who had the vision of the ladder going up into Heaven, with angels ascending and descending upon it. We too must decree concerning our Ekklesia gates—this is an open Heaven, where angels ascend and descend. A gate is an entranceway, and we are to guard the entranceways into our cities.

3. *Numbers 7:78-83*

Ahira, son of Enan, leader of the tribe of Naphtali, brought the tribe's offering for the dedication of the altar at the temple that Moses had built. We are to believe for prosperity in order to reestablish the altar of the Lord in our regions. There must be an altar of the Lord, a safe place, for people to come to God and be restored. In this new era, we will see the transfer of wealth that has been prophesied helping the Ekklesias to advance.

4. *Deuteronomy 27:13*

Naphtali is one of the tribes that stood against societal and cultural sins. Deuteronomy 27:13 tells us that the tribe of Naphtali, along with five other tribes, went up on Mount Ebal with its leaders. The Levites would call out a curse, such as, "Cursed is anyone who makes an idol," and the tribes would cry out together, "Amen!" Or, "Cursed is anyone who does not obey the word of the Lord," and the cry would come again, "Amen!" Naphtali was a tribe that raised the standard of righteousness among the people, and we are to be that voice in our regions as well.

5. *Deuteronomy 33:23*

Before his death, Moses pronounced this blessing on the tribe of Naphtali, "O Naphtali, you are rich in favor and full of the Lord's blessings; may you possess the west and the south" (NLT). We are moving into a season when the anointing and favor of God is going to be seen on the Ekklesia gates of the regions as never before. As we continue to make this era about Him, He will keep us in His unprecedented favor, a miraculous thing that only God can mantle you with. The angels of the Lord will encamp round about us ministering the favor of the Lord (see Ps. 34:7).

6. *Joshua 18:10*

"Then Joshua cast lots for them in Shiloh before the Lord, and there Joshua divided the land to the children of Israel according to their divisions" (NKJV). The tribe of Naphtali was given their geographical inheritance in Joshua 19:32-39. This was done by the casting of lots in the presence of the Lord, so it was God who chose their portion, which included 19 cities. In the book of Acts, it says that God ordains our time and place. In this season, God's apostolic hubs will also receive geographical inheritances—cities that come under their authority and that they influence for the Kingdom of God. This is a season when the Ekklesia begins to rule geographical areas, from the spirit realm, for King Jesus.

7. *Judges 5:12-18*

Naphtali was one of only two of the twelve tribes that was willing to work with the female leader Deborah. The Ekklesia must be willing to work with female leaders of God. Some of the greatest leaders in the new era that is now coming will be women of God who have faithfully served Christ and His Kingdom. The anointing of the Lord will grow and increase upon their lives, and their gifts and talents are vitally important. The true Ekklesia must embrace female leaders in order to advance forward into new times.

> SOME OF THE GREATEST LEADERS IN THE NEW ERA THAT IS NOW COMING WILL BE WOMEN OF GOD WHO HAVE FAITHFULLY SERVED CHRIST AND HIS KINGDOM.

We cannot be as the other ten tribes described in Judges 5: "In the tribe of Reuben there was great indecision. Gilead remained east of the Jordan. And why did Dan stay home? Asher sat unmoved at the seashore, remaining in his harbors. But Zebulun risked his life, as did Naphtali, on the heights of the battlefield" (Judges 5:15,17-18 NLT).

Deborah was the leader of Israel at the time and she needed help. She put out a call out to the twelve tribes and only two responded. The others did not want to submit under female leadership, but the men of Naphtali were willing to fight alongside Deborah and let her lead. This passage refers to a condemnation of the other ten tribes: Why are you sitting at home? Why aren't you willing? She needs help!

In Christ there is neither male or female (see Gal. 3:28). Both genders can, and will, be used by God.

8. Judges 6:12,16

In this passage, the angel of the Lord spoke to Gideon, calling him a mighty man of valor, and instructed him to stop the

Midianites, who had been stealing Israel's harvests for the past seven years, leaving the people impoverished. Gideon asked Naphtali and two other tribes to help him, and it simply says that their warriors responded. I love it. The tribe of Naphtali was a part of Gideon's army of 300 who fought against an enemy of 15,000.

We are here to stop lost harvests as well. I don't know how many lost harvests there have been. Joel 2:25 says He is going to restore the years the locusts, the palmerworm, cankerworm, and caterpillars have eaten away. These were grub worms that ate up harvest. I don't know how many harvests we've lost, but it has to be in the multiplied thousands. We are going to restore lost harvests in this new era.

9. *First Chronicles 12:23-38*

Naphtali trained leaders, captains, generals, and rulers. The tribe of Naphtali was unique because it was the tribe that trained generals in the Israeli army. When an Israeli soldier died in battle, his son or sons would be sent to the Naphtali tribe to be trained as generals or as leaders to take the dad's place. The Lord is saying to us today, "I want you to raise some generals for Me. I want you to train some young leaders who will replace those who have been killed in battle, or those who are no longer fighting."

The call of God is now upon us to train the coming generation who will run to battle. Those who are leaders, captains, and generals are trained differently than an ordinary soldier. The training is tougher, more intense. Leaders must be skilled in all the weapons of war and they must be fiercely loyal, dedicated, and committed to the cause. Generals cannot flinch when adversity comes.

I believe, like Naphtali, we are to train and send warriors, those who are skilled in spiritual warfare. The body of Christ is in desperate need of strong leaders and generals who will not retreat. We need leaders with backbones, not wishbones. The next move of God will not be done without them.

> WE NEED LEADERS WITH BACKBONES, NOT WISHBONES. THE NEXT MOVE OF GOD WILL NOT BE DONE WITHOUT THEM.

EVANGELISM ANGELS AND THE HARVEST

The harvest is the end of the age, and the reapers are the angels (Matthew 13:39 NKJV).

Jesus said a sign of the end times and His coming would be angels becoming reapers. Two angels are assigned to every person at birth. Their assignment is to pull out the destiny God has planned for them. Before you were ever born, God sat down and wrote your thesis—why He created you. Your two angels are briefed on that and they work to bring it out of you. You may rebel against that destiny, but the angels are not going to stop trying until you die (see Chapter Five in *Angel Armies*).

Evangelism angels help to draw destiny out of people and, of most importance, they draw you to Christ. You must be born again. There are three phases in this division.

Phase 1: The Prodigals

Millions of prodigals are about to come home. Many of them were raised in church and they know their Bible. We need to get them home and plugged in. I am convinced some of the greatest apostles, pastors, and ministers in this new era are prodigals who are returning back to the church. I list this category first because we have to have them and because there has been a billion-soul harvest prophesied. I was in Chicago a few years ago and prophesied that the greatest exodus in history would not be the exodus of the million souls Moses led out of Egyptian bondage. Rather, it would be an exodus of a billion souls leaving worldly bondage and returning to their roots in this new era.

Phase 2: New Converts

Brand-new, born-again ones are coming in. It's harvest time and evangelism angels are assisting in the harvest of new souls coming into the Kingdom of God.

Phase 3: Evangelists

The fivefold ministry office of an evangelist will be restored and connected to apostolic hubs. This office has to function and we need present-day "Billy Grahams" to come forth. The potential is unlimited and what we are about to see take place in the body of Christ is incredible.

The word *evangelism* has *angel* right in the middle of it. In the Bible, angels are God's messengers, the bearers of the good news of the gospel. The word *gospel* is the Greek word *euangelion* (which also has the word *angel* in it) and it was used in several different ways:

- Euangelion was used to announce the news of a victory. During war, Israeli runners would run back with news of how the battle was progressing. Obviously, they did not have the means of communication that we have today. If Israel had won the battle, the runner would run through the city gates to the king shouting, "Euangelion! Good news, there has been a victory."

- Euangelion was used to announce the death of an adversary. When an enemy king died, they would use euangelion—good news—to inform Israel's king, "There has been a death to your adversary."

- Euangelion was used to announce the birth of a son. Having a son meant the family's name would continue on; the family business would continue. It was good news.

- Euangelion was used to announce an upcoming wedding. Even in our times, when a couple is planning to marry, one of the first things they do is get their announcements printed. It's good news; we're having a wedding.

The word used for good news in the New Testament is the word *gospel.* We have good news, euangelion, to declare and proclaim to the world.

- Good news! There has been a victory. Calvary defeated hell's plan and Jesus has stripped the devil of his power.

- Good news! There has been a death to our adversary. Jesus destroyed principalities, powers, mights, and dominions, making a show of them openly.
- Good news! A son has been born and His Name is Jesus. The angel said, *"I bring you good tidings of great joy for unto you is born this day a Savior who is Christ the King."*
- Good news! We are heading for a wedding. The largest wedding celebration ever will be held in Heaven at the marriage supper of the Lamb.

We are beginning to see revival outbreaks in the land that will now accelerate worldwide.

A WEST VIRGINIA REVIVAL STORY

Prayer and desperation led to a great movement of God in southern West Virginia counties (March through May 2016, I think). In five weeks, 3,000 souls were saved and baptized as the fire of the Holy Spirit fell in that region. It has been called the "Coalfield Revival" and the "Appalachian Awakening."

Katie Endicott, one of the leaders of the movement, relates her story:

> Two years ago, I was driving through the mountains to school where I teach before daylight. I looked up and the mountains were on fire. I saw nothing but fire and smoke all over the place and I wondered, where were the firefighters? I got to my classroom

and the students began to remark that I smelled horrible, like smoke. I said, "Well, didn't you see all the fire on the mountains this morning?" and they said, "What fire?" I knew of another teacher who drove that same route to school so I brought her in to see if she smelled like smoke. She didn't see the fire either. The Holy Spirit stopped me, sat me down, and told me that soon revival fire was going to fall from Heaven in our area.

I was overwhelmed and blessed because this is an area that has really been consecrated in prayer throughout many generations. This had been decades in the making. People have been praying for this their entire lives. People like my dad, a pastor, who would wake at 4 a.m., go to the church, and pray for revival. My grandparents and great grandparents who prayed for revival their entire lives.

On March 24, Skyler Miller, a football player at Logan County High School, was boldly led of God to preach in the school hallway after lunch. Skyler had been healed of leukemia twice and gave his life to Christ after the first healing. Students listened to him that day and some repented of their sins and invited Jesus Christ to be their Lord and Savior.

On April 10, a three-day revival was held at the Regional Church of God in Delbarton, a coal mining town of 1,237 people. The following week, the evangelist Matt Hartley was invited to speak at the high school prayer club. Normally they have about 30 students, but on this day 400 students came and 150 were saved. This is when the revival really began. The prayer club then held a student-led worship event at the football field and 3,000 people came. The service lasted for four hours and hundreds came forward to be saved and many were baptized in an inflatable pool that night.

Also, during this period of time a group of students left the prayer club, got on the bus to go home, and the Spirit of God fell on the bus and many received the Holy Spirit.

The Holy Ghost fell in a fourth grade class room and tears flowed as the students felt the strong presence of Jesus.

One woman was awakened at 4 a.m. and said the Holy Spirit told her to give her life to God right then. She hadn't been to church in 13 years. Many of her family members have come to Christ as a result of what happened to her that night.

A young wife testified that her husband had gotten saved; she had been praying for him for months. He received Jesus into his life through some men at work on a Monday morning.

At Mingo Central High School, prayer has replaced profanity in the hallways. A group meets every morning at the flag pole to read scripture and pray.

Many, many young people have given their testimonies of coming to the Lord and their lives being changed.

A fireman testifies of attending the revival and being saved, and then he invited a Williamson city clerk to go and he got saved.

The evangelist has been interviewed by CBN News and said, "This is not man-made. This is the presence of God that is overwhelming us, that is being released upon hungry people that are tired of stagnant Christianity and 'safe' church. They want Jesus more than anything else."

On what ended up being the last night of this revival, the visiting evangelist shared from Jeremiah 8:20, "The harvest is past, the summer is ended, and we are not saved."

They sang an old revival song from 1842: *"O Why Not Tonight."*

> *Oh do not let the word depart*
>
> *And close thine eyes against the light;*
>
> *Poor sinner, harden not your*
> *heart, be saved, oh, tonight*
>
> *O why not tonight, O why not tonight*
>
> *Wilt thou be said? Then why not tonight.*

A mother let out a strong, loud scream and many rushed over to her to see what was wrong. There was nothing wrong—her seven-year-old daughter had just given her heart to the Lord!

Psalm 126:5-6 says, "Those who plant in tears will harvest with shouts of joy. They weep as they go to plant their seed, but they sing as they return with the harvest" (NLT).

Our area was devastated by the economy and by drugs. It was overwhelming and people were losing hope. But this revival has given hope. It has turned everything around. People are excited, passionate, they have joy, and they have hope. You can't go anywhere without hearing what God is doing. It is what we have always believed for. We always knew that the Lord was going to send true revival and true awakening to southern West Virginia. There has never been anything like this.

REVIVAL SPARKS

There are reports of revival "outbreaks" all over the world. Recently, in Lynchburg, Virginia, a local church experienced an outpouring of the presence of the Lord for about eight weeks that included many healings, many being saved, and then receiving the baptism of the Holy Spirit.

In Koreatown, Los Angeles, another church hosted a 21-day revival unlike any they had ever experienced before. It primarily focused on the coming generation, including millennials and Generation Z. There was a hunger for more of God, and the revival was experienced online as well, with many receiving dreams and visitations and impartation, the same as the ones physically present in the meetings.

> Recently, "The Send," founded by Lou Engle, was hosted in Brasilia, Brazil. Nearly 140,000 attended this meeting, including Brazilian President Jair Bolsonaro. The event was spread out at three stadiums and an additional 1.7 million watched via livestream. This meeting was coordinated with several other ministries, and they [Andy Byrd, Youth with a Mission] stated "the outpouring of healing, miracles, signs and wonders was mind-blowing. This whole event was about the exultation of Jesus and the empowerment of the next generation to change the world."
>
> In 2019 The Send drew around 60,000 in Orlando, Florida, with another 250,000 watching online.

There are reports of revivals occurring in Argentina, England, Australia—all across the land.

These are just a small example of what God has done and is continuing to do. There is a glory revival that is coming and will be far greater than anything we have seen in recent history.

IT IS TIME!

We are now moving into the greatest evangelistic era the church has ever seen. Evangelism and harvest angels are assisting Holy Spirit and the true Ekklesia to reap the billion-soul harvest. We will now see millions of prodigals coming back to Father's House. We will see hundreds of millions of new converts. Fiery evangelists will now rise to proclaim the gospel of the Kingdom. Many of them are from the coming generation. We are moving toward miraculous harvest.

DECREES

1. WE DECREE the magnificent communicators are rising.

2. WE DECREE we are watchmen on the gates of our cities; no anti-Christ agendas.

3. WE DECREE the Ekklesia will prosper and wealth will be transferred.

4. WE DECREE a standard of righteousness will be seen in our land.

5. WE DECREE the favor of the Lord is growing on the body of Christ.

6. WE DECREE the Ekklesia will begin to rule its geographical areas for King Jesus.

7. WE DECREE that female leaders will now rise and be accepted for the gifts they bring to the body of Christ.

8. WE DECREE our lost harvests are being restored.

9. WE DECREE great leaders from the coming generation are rising to take their place in the King's Ekklesia.

10. WE DECREE break up, break out, break through, passover, and possess.

Chapter 12

DIVISIONS OF ANGELS AND THE EKKLESIA

Multiple divisions of angel armies are now being sent to earth to assist an emerging and strong Ekklesia of King Jesus, a church that embraces the opportunity to reign with Him in this life (see Rom. 5:17). Holy Spirit is in charge of this campaign and is now beginning times of refreshing and out-pourings of anointings to empower the heirs to function in His Kingdom, as intended. We have now entered a new-era Pentecost, greater than Acts 2, when replenishing anointings, one after the other, wave after wave, will continue to energize the glorious church, as promised. We have moved into the season when mighty surges of Holy Spirit power will invigo-rate Christ's Kingdom on the earth. Supernatural activity that has been seen throughout the ages in certain times and sea-sons will accelerate in full measure. We will now see a people who represent Jesus as He truly is, doing the same works as He did.

The divisions of angel armies are here to assist the people of God in serving that high purpose. I believe it is why, when

Holy Spirit began to reveal angel armies to me years ago, one of His first statements was, "I will now lead another campaign on earth for King Jesus. It will be far greater than the one I led in Acts chapter 2 to birth the New Testament church. But this time, I will be bringing far more of the angel armies. The greatest days in church history are not in your past; they are in your present and in your future." We are moving into the awesome days we've been promised. Holy Spirit is leading the way and divisions of His powerful angel armies are assisting us to accomplish the new campaign here on earth. There has never been anything like it before. A global outpouring of Holy Spirit on a functioning spiritual Kingdom around the world is now being poured out.

WE ARE MOVING INTO THE AWESOME DAYS WE'VE BEEN PROMISED.

Remember, Holy Spirit spoke to me concerning a new-era decade of greater glory and a special Pentecost that has now fully come. Here is that word:

> It is now in its moment. This year, the Ekklesia leaves its training and begins deployment. This will be a year of deployment and change for your future. The functioning Ekklesia will rise to operate in higher authority and its advance will be rapid. The world will see the deployment of Heaven's Kingdom Ekklesia and angel armies. This will suddenly and aggressively

be revealed. Strongholds of hell will be broken and iniquitous roots will dry up under its superior power, authority, and administered justice. The withering of hell's kingdom will begin to be seen in indisputable ways. For the heirs of Kingdom authority are being seated in their regional spheres of influence and their angels, along with the divisions of angels assisting them, are aligning with the assigning. You will now see a clear merger; Heaven and earth will merge in unified oneness of purpose to escalate the King's victories, expand His Kingdom, and implement His spiritual Kingdom's government. The merger of the earth realm with the spirit realm will surge in visible function in this new Pentecost era.

Then I heard Holy Spirit say, "The purposes and plans for this era have fully come and will not be reversed. It is an immutable decree of King Jesus for His Ekklesia."

That was an unusual statement to have heard. Whenever you hear Holy Spirit use unusual phrasing, pay attention, because there's a reason for doing so. The immutable oath of God's promise is talked about in Hebrews 6. It speaks to a decision that is relentlessly determined to be done, based on the nature and character, abilities and reputation of the one who makes the oath. The immutable oath is decreed seven times; it is a complete, full oath. It was said of the one making the oath that they have seven'd themselves.

For men indeed swear by the greater, and an oath for confirmation is for them an end of all dispute. Thus God, determining to show more abundantly to the heirs of promise the immutability of His counsel, confirmed it by an oath, that by two immutable things, in which it is impossible for God to lie, we might have strong consolation, who have fled for refuge to lay hold of the hope set before us (Hebrews 6:16-18 NKJV).

The Greek word for *immutable* is *ametathetos*, meaning unchangeable (Strong's G276). Holy Spirit was saying to me there are aspects of this new era in which King Jesus has seven'd Himself, swearing they will be implemented, they will be done. He is swearing to His own involvement. The King Himself says there are facets in this new season that are unchangeable for His Ekklesia—those who are pursuing a higher level and raising the bar to new boundaries and territories He has put before them.

This is the era of the Kingdom of God's Ekklesia on the earth, also referred to as the glorious church era. He's returning for a glorious church and it's going to happen sometime, so why couldn't it happen now? This is the season when the glorious church era begins and we enter into the new boundaries that have been set. Holy Spirit says, "The purposes and the plans have fully come and they will not be reversed." It is an immutable decree of King Jesus for His true Ekklesia. This is its "prepared for" moment—the right time, the right era. Our King has sworn both His and His Kingdom's assistance, as well as angelic participation. He has seven'd Himself to rise and fulfill the prophetic word of Micah 2:13, running before His Kingdom Ekklesia, ensuring that they will break through.

This is the decade when the King will make His stand on the earth, assisting us to break through the obstacles of hell and the strongholds of darkness. The Ekklesia, empowered with Holy Spirit and with angelic assistance, will break through and demolish warped philosophies and doctrines of devils. In this magnificent era, barrier walls will be smashed by the decrees of the King's Ekklesia as it begins to aggressively function as He has sworn it will.

The King, the Breaker Himself, will put His Ekklesia on His shoulders and run with them. Think about that. It's not about whether or not *we* can do it; it's about whether or not *He* can do it. He swears, "I'm going to do it. I'm going to bust up roadblocks, move mountains, and break you through. You're going to be who I say you are, who I have prepared you to be. You are going to do what I've said you will do. I give My oath that the gates of hell will not prevail against My Ekklesia. All the powers of hell combined will not overcome you. It's unchangeable; no compromises, mutations, or appeasing doctrines. I stake My reputation on it. It's immutable."

IT'S NOT ABOUT WHETHER OR NOT *WE* CAN DO IT; IT'S ABOUT WHETHER OR NOT *HE* CAN DO IT.

When Holy Spirit added those two words, "it's immutable," it resonated deep inside of me. If He had just said that the purposes and plans for your time have fully come, I would have rejoiced in that. But He didn't stop there. He added, "It's

ANGEL ARMIES ON ASSIGNMENT

immutable." It's an *unchangeable* decree of the King for His Ekklesia. We have a responsibility, but the weight is on His shoulders, not ours. That understanding sets our focus on what the Ekklesia can decree and live by—we are to say what He says. It's not our declaration of purpose but His. Our decrees are powerful, but His decrees go to another whole level, raising the bar. He has given His immutable oath, which brings a deeper awareness to us that He can handle it.

The Lord says:

> When My Ekklesia decides to raise the bar, I am going to raise the yoke-destroying anointing, as promised. I'll make My stand with you, running before the decrees that you're making in My Name. My Kingdom will advance before you. Angels of breakthrough will accompany Me in order to penetrate the territories that you have soaked with My words of promise. They will break up entrenched powers of darkness in both the natural and the spirit realms, and you will break through. My Ekklesia's time and era of breakthrough has fully come; you have crossed the line of demarcation. Rise with Me and run, as My true Ekklesia, through doors of hope, opportunity, advancement, and breakthrough.

The prophets are calling this decade the roaring 20s. Get ready because the real remnant, the true church, is in for the ride of their lives. There's a determination of our King Jesus that is going to be seen in this decade. He knows how to set

His face like a flint and He is doing that now, in our times. He has fire in His eyes and a sword in His hand.

As I was praying about all of this, I said, "Holy Spirit, tell me about this season. Talk to me about this period of time." Then I just started listening. A word rose up inside of my spirit that I heard so clearly, and it was a word I don't think I've ever talked about before. I heard this statement: "The keystone is being raised into place." That was not what I was expecting to hear. I don't know that I've ever even thought about that. Again, it's important to pay attention to unusual phrasing of the Holy Spirit.

The keystone is a stone at the top of a crown or an arch that locks all the other pieces together in a building. It's the stabilizing stone on which the beams lean against, to hold them in place. The weight of the beams leaning against the keystone holds it all in position.

Buildings with arch systems will collapse if there's no keystone. The keystone is the support system of a structure; without it, the building falls apart. Today, the word *keystone* has come to mean the central part of a policy, plan, mission, or process on which all else depends and is held together.

A keystone references the most strategic part. Holy Spirit had said, "The keystone is being raised in place." Pentecost is a keystone of the church. So much depended and leaned on it that Jesus commanded His disciples in Acts 1:4, "Don't leave Jerusalem without it. Don't leave until you receive the promise of the Father, because you can't do what you need to do without it. You can't do it in the natural. It will have to come through spiritual means." World evangelism and the discipling of nations depend upon it. The structural beam of the true church leans upon and is supported by a new-era Pentecost. It's locked into position by outpourings of the Spirit and by what occurs at Pentecost.

Holy Spirit and His keystone anointing are central to everything that we do. Signs, wonders, and miracles are dependent upon it. His fresh new Pentecost and outpouring of power is the key to our mission and assignment. It's His presence, His power, His leadership, and His anointing upon which everything else rests. Without it, everything falls apart.

A fresh, new Pentecost activates cohesion, a stabilizing force that is going to fill the New Testament church of our times. This outpouring is going to begin to hold things together, lock it all in place, and activate a building that we call church. It won't be a building made with hands—we are going to be a live building.

I believe we are now moving into this literal new Pentecost, an incredible outpouring of the Holy Spirit. This will be the largest activation in all of church history, and it is due now. Our God's prevailing anointing of favor is going to soak the people of God, the true church, and we are going to see the greatest move of God that has ever been seen on the earth.

All of the streams and all of the moves revealed from Acts 2 until now—everything they individually emphasized, all they taught, all the doctrines they restored, all they meant and established—are now being raised up to lean in place against the keystone, aligned into a new Pentecost. All of them will now function, held together and anointed to succeed by what I can only call a mega outpouring of Holy Spirit.

There is no crisis in the natural realm that can stop it. It will only backfire on hell because the anointing is going to turn things in our favor. It's not that we don't go through crises, because we do. It's not that tough times don't come against us, because they will. It's not that confinement and activities of darkness don't attack us, but we are anointed with favor. The anointing of our God and King, Holy Spirit and His Kingdom, will simply begin to cycle us from barrenness to greater productivity. Greater is He that is in us than He that is in the world (see 1 John 4:4).

> ## THERE IS NO CRISIS IN THE NATURAL REALM THAT CAN STOP IT. IT WILL ONLY BACKFIRE ON HELL BECAUSE THE ANOINTING IS GOING TO TURN THINGS IN OUR FAVOR.

This is actually the teaching of the New Testament apostles. It is most certainly what the apostle Paul taught the Philippians, writing to them from jail—a place of confinement—which was his punishment for preaching the gospel of Jesus Christ. He shared some principles that I believe connect some of the dots for us prophetically today. Philippians 1:12 says that this will only cause a furtherance of the gospel. Paul said his imprisonment, along with everything else that had happened to him, had resulted in some of the believers becoming bolder than they ever had been in declaring the gospel of King Jesus. He also said concerning himself that it resulted in his being able to present the gospel of the Kingdom to ethnic groups that he ordinarily would not have been able to do, actually furthering the gospel. Paul then said in Philippians 1:19 that this will actually turn for our deliverance.

I love this in *The Message* Bible: In Philippians 1:20, Paul states, "They didn't shut me up; they gave me a pulpit!"

Paul also wrote in Philippians 1:6, while in confinement, that he was headed for "a flourishing finish." That's a man of faith. This should inspire us and speak to us. A mega outpouring is beginning to build. The keystone holding it all together is being raised and the true church, the remnant warriors, is headed for a flourishing finish. Your purpose and destiny is headed for a flourishing finish. You are cycling right now into your most productive period. You will now see birthed on this planet what we couldn't birth on our own. The divisions of angels sent by Holy Spirit are going to help us finish well. They are going to help us break up, break out, break through, passover, and possess a glorious future. We are moving forward from a literal Pentecost into surge after surge of replenishing outpourings from Heaven. The remnant will be soaked with power from on high. Our greatest days are in front of us!

DECREES

1. WE DECREE Holy Spirit is leading another campaign, greater than Acts 2, for King Jesus.

2. WE DECREE the purpose and plans for this New Era cannot be reversed. It is immutable.

3. WE DECREE the strongholds of hell will be broken and iniquitous roots will dry up. It is immutable.

4. WE DECREE the divisions of angel armies are aligning with the assignments of Holy Spirit.

5. WE DECREE angel armies are on assignment.

6. WE DECREE the keystone has been raised and the support structure for a New Era Pentecost is in place.

7. WE DECREE a mega outpouring of the Holy Spirit has begun.

8. WE DECREE there is no crisis in the natural realm that can stop this move of God.

9. WE DECREE the greatest days in church history are not in our past; they are in our present and in our future.

10. WE DECREE break up, break out, break through, passover, and possess.

BIBLIOGRAPHY

James Strong, *The New Strong's Exhaustive Concordance of the Bible* (Nashville, TN: Thomas Nelson Publishers, 1990).

Spiros Zodhiates, *The Complete Word Study Old Testament* (Chattanooga, TN: AMG Publishers, 1994).

Spiros Zodhiates, *The Complete Word Study New Testament* (Chattanooga, TN: AMG Publishers, 1991).

ABOUT DR. TIM SHEETS

Dr. Tim Sheets is an apostle, pastor of The Oasis Church, the founder of Awakening Now Prayer Network, and author. He travels extensively throughout the nations, carrying his heart and vision for awakening and reformation, the coming generation, and releasing an anointing for signs, wonders, and miracles. He and his wife, Carol, reside in Lebanon, Ohio.

CONTACT INFORMATION

www.timsheets.org
Tim Sheets Ministries,
6927 Lefferson Road,
Middletown, Ohio. 45044
carol@timsheets.org
513-424-7150

Facebook: facebook.com/ApostleTimSheets
Instagram: @TimDSheets

Jackie S. (2/1/2021 (MON)

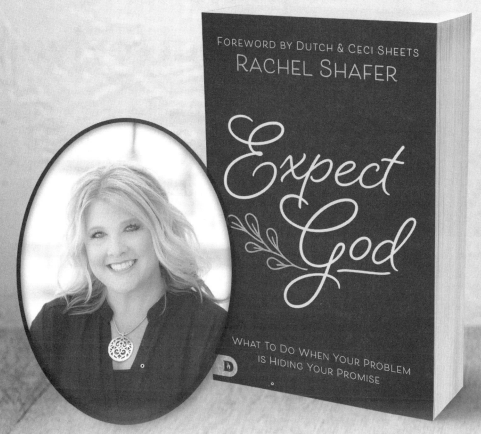